Historical Perspectives
from a
Nation Divided:

Richmond to Appomattox

BLUE MUSTANG
P R E S S
Blue Mustang Press
Boston, Massachusetts

First printing

ISBN 978-1-935199-05-2
PUBLISHED BY BLUE MUSTANG PRESS
www.BlueMustangPress.com
Boston, Massachusetts

Printed in the United States of America

Historical Perspectives from a Nation Divided:
Richmond to Appomattox

Reprinting in their entirety:

The Falling Flag
EVACUATION OF RICHMOND, RETREAT AND
SURRENDER AT APPOMATTOX
By
EDWARD M. BOYKIN,
LT. COL. 7th REG'T S.C. CAVALRY
Published in 1874

and

The Fourth Massachusetts Cavalry in the Closing Scenes
of the War for the Maintenance of the Union, from
Richmond to Appomatox
as told by Various Authors

and reprinting selections from the 1866 edition of:
War Poetry of the South
Edited By
William Gilmore Simms, LL. D.

Introduction to this Series of Books

This series of books, "Historical Perspectives from a Nation Divided" seeks to offer different - often contemporary - views of related historical events. In general, as this topic lends itself to such divisions, the differing perspectives will be that of North and South.

There is a great wealth of histories, recollections, regimental diaries, and other such types of published works relating to the people and operations of the American Civil War that were written by the then-living doers of those deeds. The surge in such writings, starting immediately after the War's end and peaking in the early years of the 20th century (when these writers were facing their own mortality) has left us with countless recountings of similar events. This series hopes to bring many of those texts back to those who find interest in them, both on an entertainment level and on a research level.

It is worth noting that often the writer of a piece may, at the time of writing, have different convictions than when the events took place. Someone who lived and fought in the CSA may, 40 years later, be living comfortably in Boston or New York and grown to dismiss actions taken earlier as the errors of youth. These occurances are telling as well and interesting in the extreme as we see perceptions of history altering within the same person over time.

Lucien Febvre said that "History is the daughter of Time" and that adage is well represented within the texts reprinted in this series. Even more apparent within the texts, particularly those written soon after the War ended, is what Mark Twain said about history: "The very ink with which all history is written is merely fluid prejudice."

These beliefs are well represented in the works published here and it's an unquestioned value that these treasures still exist to provide a window into the construction of history.

The Falling Flag

EVACUATION OF RICHMOND, RETREAT AND SURRENDER AT APPOMATTOX

By
EDWARD M. BOYKIN,
LT. COL. 7th REG'T S.C. CAVALRY

This text is taken from the Third Edition of the book, published by in 1874 by:

E.J. HALE & SON, PUBLISHERS,
MURRAY STREET.
New York

A CAVALRY CHARGE.

DEDICATION

TO THE OFFICERS AND MEN OF THE 7th South Carolina Cavalry, THIS SHORT ACCOUNT OF AN INTERESTING PERIOD IN THEIR MILITARY HISTORY, AND THAT OF THE CAUSE THEY LOVED SO WELL, AND FOR WHICH THEY FOUGHT SO FAITHFULLY, Is Dedicated, BY ONE WHO CONSIDERS HAVING BEEN THEIR COMRADE THE PROUDEST RECOLLECTION OF HIS LIFE.

PREFACE.

The writer only attempts to give some account of what occurred within his own observation; he would have esteemed it a privilege to enter into all the detail that lights up the last desperate struggle, made by that glorious remnant of the Army of Northern Virginia, with its skeleton battalions from every Southern State; illustrating their own fame and that of their noble leader, mile by mile, on that weary march from Richmond to Appomattox.

But he has confined himself to his own experiences, and in a great measure to what happened to his own Brigade, because it was written out, immediately after the war, from that standpoint. And if there be any merit in it, it is simply as a journal—what one man saw, and the impression produced thereby. This, even within a limited range, if truly put, represents at least a phase of the last act in the bloody drama that had been enacting for four years. More than this he could not hope to do, but leaves to abler hands the greater task that swells the current of events into the full tide of history.

Camden, South Carolina,
June 15th, 1874.

EVACUATION OF RICHMOND, 1865.

On Saturday, the 1st day of April, 1865, orders reached us at camp
headquarters of the Seventh South Carolina Cavalry, Gary's Brigade, to
send forward all the dismounted men of the regiment to report to Lt. Col.
Barham, Twenty-fourth Regiment Virginia Cavalry, in command of
dismounted men of the brigade, for duty on the lines. Began to think that
a move was intended of some sort, but on the brink, as all knew and felt
for some time, of great events, it was difficult to say what was expected.
On Sunday, the 2d, about mid-day, orders came for the wagon train of the
brigade, spare horses, baggage of all sorts, that was to go at all—the
greater part was to be left—to move into Richmond at once, and fall into
the general train of the army of the north bank of the James River.
Richmond then was to be evacuated, so all felt, though no public
statement of the fact had been made; heavy fighting had been going on
during the day, in the neighborhood of Petersburg, but there had been
one unceasing roar of battle around us for months, and no particular
account was taken of that.

The brigade was ordered to move after nightfall from its position (our
winter quarters) between the Williamsburg and the "Nine Mile" road,
about four miles from Richmond, and immediately behind the outer line
of works on the edge of the battle field of the "Seven Pines."

We moved after dark—the Seventh South Carolina, Col. Haskell; the
Hampton Legion, South Carolina, Lieut. Col. Arnold; the Twenty-fourth
Virginia, Col. Robbins, and a small party of the Seventh Georgia, part of a
company only—Gen. Gary commanding the brigade.

The Seventh Georgia were, with the exception spoken of, dismounted,
though belonging to our brigade. We halted on the Charles City road,
found all the infantry gone; Gen. Longstreet, who commanded on the

15

north bank, had been withdrawn with Gen. Field's Division across the river, to reinforce Gen. Lee around Petersburg, some two or three days before, leaving only the Division of Gen. Kershaw in our immediate neighborhood, and Gen. Custis Lee in command of the Marine Brigade and City Reserves, next the river, near Fort Gilmer, all under the command of Lt. Gen. Ewell; also Hankin's Battery, Virginia, attached to our brigade.

We were to wait until two o'clock, and as soon as our dismounted men, who were filling the place of infantry pickets withdrawn, should come in, we were to move on to the city, acting as "rear guard," and burn Mayo's Bridge. It was all out now; there had been a heavy fight in the morning, near Petersburg, Gen. Lee all but overwhelmed, Gen. A.P. Hill killed, and the army in full retreat on Burkville, to effect, if possible, a junction with Gen. Johnston, in North Carolina.

We built big fires of brush wood, to give light and warmth, and deceive the enemy. It was cold, though in April; the men, as usual, light-hearted and cheerful round the fires, though an empire was passing away around them; some, with an innate consciousness of the work before them, when they heard that the halt was to be for two or three hours, wrapped in their overcoats, with the capes drawn over their heads, were soon sound asleep, forgetting the defeat of armies, the work of yesterday, the toil and danger of to-morrow, in some quiet dream of a home perhaps never seen again.

Two o'clock came and passed; our men had not come in. The General waited until four o'clock. I think we were at this point six miles from Richmond. We should have been there at daylight, and we were to burn the bridge in time to prevent the enemy's crossing, as our whole train, with infantry and artillery, had crossed during the night. Our brigade of cavalry, and one company of artillery attached to it, were all that were on this side—the north bank of the river. We could wait no longer, and moved off slowly. In a short time after we started a tremendous explosion took place toward the river, lighting up everything like day, and waking every echo, and every Yankee for thirty miles around. It was evidently a gunboat on the river at "Drury's Bluff." Two others followed, but they did not equal the first. She was iron-clad—the "Virginia," as we afterwards heard—just completed. She burst like a bomb-shell, and told, in anything but a whisper, the desperate condition of things. There was no time to be lost; the Yankees had heard it as well as ourselves, and we moved on at once.

We overtook, just at daylight, and passed a small squad of our dismounted men from the Seventh, who had got in from the picket line. When we reached the intermediate line of works, where the "Charles City" and "New Kent" roads come together, not far from the "turnpike gate," which all who travelled that road—and who of the army of Northern Virginia did not?—will remember, the sun was just rising, and an ugly red glare showed itself in the direction of Richmond that dimmed the early sunshine.

At this point the General determined (though expecting the enemy's cavalry every moment) to occupy the works, and wait for the dismounted men. The guns of the battery that accompanied us were placed in position, and our men dismounted and occupied the lines on the right and left of the road. In about a half hour's time, and to our great satisfaction—for it seemed a hard case to leave the poor tired fellows to be gobbled up—a straggling line of tired men and poor walkers, as dismounted cavalry always must be in their big boots and spurs, showed themselves over the hill, dragged themselves along, and passed on before us into the city. We followed on, went down the steep hill by the house where General Johnston's headquarters were about the time of the retreat from Yorktown, and got into the river road, and so had the enemy behind us. It was here he might have cut us off from the city and secured the bridge.

We passed into the "Rockets," the southern suburb of Richmond, at an easy marching gait, and there learned that the bridge had taken fire from some of the buildings, which by this time we could see were on fire in the city. Fearing our retreat would be cut off at that point, which would throw us from our position as rear-guard, we pushed on rapidly, the column moving at a trot through the "Rockets."

The peculiar population of that suburb were gathered on the sidewalk; bold, dirty looking women, who had evidently not been improved by four years' military association, dirtier (if possible) looking children, and here and there skulking, scoundrelly looking men, who in the general ruin were sneaking from the holes they had been hiding in—not, though, in

17

the numbers that might have been expected, for the great crowd, as we soon saw, were hard at it, pillaging the burning city. One strapping virago stood on the edge of the pavement with her arms akimbo, looking at us with intense scorn as we swept along; I could have touched her with the toe of my boot as I rode by her, closing the rear of the column; she caught my eye—"Yes," said she, with all of Tipperary in her brogue, "afther fighting them for four years ye're running like dawgs!" The woman was either drunk or very much in earnest, for I give her credit for feeling all she said, and her son or husband had to do his own fighting, I will answer for it, wherever he was, or get no kiss or comfort from her. But I could not stop to explain that General Longstreet's particular orders were not to make a fight in the city, if it could be avoided, so I left her to the enjoyment of her own notions, unfavorable as they evidently were to us.

On we went across the creek, leaving a picket at that point to keep a lookout for the enemy, that we knew must now be near upon our heels. It was after seven o'clock, the sun having been up for some time. After getting into Main street and passing the two tobacco warehouses opposite one another, occupied as prisons in the early years of the war, we met the motley crowd thronging the pavement, loaded with every species of plunder.

Bare-headed women, their arms filled with every description of goods, plundered from warehouses and shops, their hair hanging about their ears, were rushing one way to deposit their plunder and return for more, while a current of the empty-handed surged in a contrary direction towards the scene.

The roaring and crackling of the burning houses, the trampling and snorting of our horses over the paved streets as we swept along, wild sounds of every description, while the rising sun came dimly through the cloud of smoke that hung like a pall around him, made up a scene that beggars description, and which I hope never to see again—the saddest of many of the sad sights of war—a city undergoing pillage at the hands of its own mob, while the standards of an empire were being taken from its capitol, and the tramp of a victorious enemy could be heard at its gates.

Richmond had collected within its walls the refuse of the war—thieves and deserters, male and female, the vilest of the vile were there, but strict military discipline had kept it down. Now, in one moment, it was all removed—all restraint was taken off—and you may imagine the consequences. There were said to be 5,000 deserters in the city, and you could see the grey jackets here and there sprinkled in the mob that was roaring down the street. When we reached somewhere between Twentieth and Twenty-fifth streets—I will not be certain—the flames swept across Main street so we could not pass. The column turned to the right, and so got into the street above it. On this (Franklin street) are many private residences; at the windows we could see the sad and tearful faces of the kind Virginia women, who had never failed the soldier in four long years of war and trouble, ready to the last to give him devoted attendance in his wounds and sickness, and to share with his necessities the last morsel.

These are strong but not exaggerated expressions. Thousands, yes, tens of thousands, from the Rio Grande to the Potomac, can bear witness to the truth of everything I say. And it was a sad thought to every man that was there that day, that we seemed, as a compensation for all that they had done for us, to be leaving them to the mercy of the enemy; but their own General Lee was gone before, and we were but as the last wave of the receding tide.

After getting round the burning square we turned back towards the river. The portion of Mayo's, or rather the lesser bridge that crossed the canal, had taken fire from the large flouring mill near it, and was burning, but not the main bridge; so we followed the cross street below the main approach to the bridge, at the foot of which was a bridge across the canal, forcing our horses through the crowd of pillagers gathered at this point, greater than at any other—they had broken into some government stores. A low white man—he seemed a foreigner—was about to strike a woman over a barrel of flour under my horse's nose, when a stout negro took her part and threatened to throw him into the canal. We were the rear regiment at this time. All this occurred at one of those momentary halts to which the rear of a marching column is subjected; in another moment we moved on, the crowd closed in, and we saw no more. After crossing the canal we were obliged to go over a stone conduit single file.

At last we were on the main bridge, along which were scattered faggots to facilitate the burning. Lieut. Cantey, Sergt. Lee and twenty men from the Seventh were left, under the supervision of Colonel Haskell, to burn the bridge, while the rest went slowly up the hill on which Manchester is built, and waited for them. Just as the canal bridge on which we had crossed took fire, about forty of Kautz' cavalry galloped easily up Main street, fired a long shot with their carbines on the party at the bridge, but went on up the street instead of coming down to the river. They were too late to secure the bridge, if that had been their object, which they seemed to be aware of, as they made no attempt to do so. Their coming was of service to the city. General Ord, as we afterwards understood, acted with promptness and kindness, put down the mob, and put out the fire, and protected the people of Richmond from the mob and his own soldiers, in their persons and property.

As we sat upon our horses on the high hill on which Manchester is built, we looked down upon the City of Richmond. By this time the fire appeared to be general. Some magazine or depot for the manufacture of ordnance stores was on fire about the centre of the city; it was marked by the peculiar blackness of smoke; from the middle of it would come the roar of bursting shells and boxes of fixed ammunition, with flashes that gave it the appearance of a thunder cloud of huge proportions with lightning playing through it. On our right was the navy yard, at which were several steamers and gunboats on fire, and burning in the river, from which the cannon were thundering as the fire reached them. The old war-scarred city seemed to prefer annihilation to conquest—a useless sacrifice, as it afterwards proved, however much it may have added to the grandeur of the closing scene; but such is war.

Moving slowly out of Manchester, we soon got among the host of stragglers, who, from a natural fear of the occupation of the towns both of Petersburg and Richmond, were going with the rear of our army. Civilians, in some cases ladies of gentle nurture, without means of conveyance, were sitting on their trunks by the roadside—refugees from Petersburg to Richmond a few days before, now refugees from Richmond into the highway; indeed the most were from Petersburg, driven out literally by the artillery fire. The residents of Richmond, as a general thing, remained.

Two ladies here got into our regimental ambulance, rode for a few miles, and then took refuge in some farm house, I suppose, as they disappeared before the day was over.

By the roadside, or rather the sidewalk, were sitting on their bags some hardy, weather-beaten looking men. They were what was left of the crew of the "famous Alabama," and had just landed from the gunboats that had been blown up on the river, which had first started us on our march. Admiral Semmes was with them; I remember some of our young men jesting with the bronzed veterans, but we did not then know the renowned Captain of the great Confederate war ship was there in person, or he certainly should not have had to complain of being left standing in the road and dusted by the "young rascals of the cavalry rear-guard," as he does in his book. Some one of the "young cavalry rascals" would have been dismounted, and his horse given to the man who had carried our flag so far and fought it so well.

Acting as rear-guard, we moved very slowly, giving time for all stragglers, wagons and worn out artillery horses to close up. Already we began to come upon a piece of artillery mired down, the horses dead beat, the gun left, and the horses double-teamed into the remaining pieces. So we went into camp that night, after marching all day, only eleven miles from Richmond, on the "Burkville road." Burkville is the point at which the railroad branches west to Lynchburg and south to Danville, and was our objective point.

The brigade went into camp, or bivouac rather, by squadrons, in a piece of woods, the men picketing their horses immediately behind their camp fires. The fires burned brightly, the horses ate the corn the men had brought in their bags and what forage they could get hold of during the day. Our surgeon, Dr. McLaurin, had gotten up his ambulance, and helped out our bread and bacon with a cup of coffee and some not very salt James River herring, that he had among his stores—and so ended the first day's march.

We did not move until nearly nine o'clock next morning, as at our slowest marching gait we out-travelled the march we were covering. The day was spent in following after the movements of the army. Occasional pieces of artillery left upon the roadside showed that the horses were giving out. After dark we crossed the Appomattox, some twenty or twenty-five miles from Richmond, at the railroad bridge, which was planked over so our horses could cross. After crossing the river we went into camp about a mile beyond, surrounded by most of the infantry of the north bank, General Longstreet's immediate command, the men leading their horses over. One of the young men attached to our mess, a good looking young fellow, had his pockets filled with ham and biscuits near the crossing by some good Samaritan he had met, and so our herring, grilled by one of the couriers on the half of a canteen, was helped out by this addition.

We were suddenly roused in the night by a fire in the dry grass on which we were sleeping. It caught from our camp fire and was among our blankets before we knew it. There was a general jumping up and stamping it out. One of the men created quite a sensation by shaking his India rubber, which was on fire; it flew to pieces in a shower of flame. The effect of the night attack is still shown in the blistered and scorched condition of my field-glasses. We were at this point but a few miles from Amelia Court House, between which and our camp of that night the road from Petersburg joins the road from Richmond, and the two columns respectively met—the two streams flowed into one—forming what was left of Lee's great army of Northern Virginia—the men exchanging in the fresh morning air kindly greetings with one another, from Texas to Maryland, from the Potomac to the Rio Grande. They marched along, leaving their fate in the hands of the great leader they knew so well and had trusted so long.

About a mile or two from Amelia Court House our brigade was ordered to graze their horses in a clover field, still keeping the regiments together as near as could be in squadrons, for we could make no calculations, as will be seen, upon the movements of the enemy's cavalry. Colonel Haskell, Colonel Robbins, of the Twenty-fourth Virginia, and myself were seated upon the steps of an old house, breakfasting with Colonel Robbins, who had been fortunate enough to meet a friend who had filled his haversack, and shared his good luck with us, watching the men and horses who were eating what they could get, when here it came at last: "Mount the brigade and move up at once!" The enemy had gotten in force between us and Burkville, and his cavalry had struck our wagon and ordnance train some three or four miles from where we were. So there was mounting in hot haste, and off we went at a gallop.

We soon reached the point they had first attacked and set fire to the wagons—the canvas covers taking fire very easily. Their plan of operation seemed to be to strike the train, which was several miles long at a given point, fire as many wagons as their number admitted of doing at once, then making a circuit and striking it again, leaving an intermediate point untouched.

We did not suppose the troops actually engaged in the firing exceeded three or four hundred well mounted men, but had a large body of cavalry moving parallel with them in easy supporting distance. This was a very effectual mode of throwing the march of the wagon train into confusion, independent of the absolute destruction they caused.

The burning caissons, as we rode by, were anything but pleasant neighbors, and were exploding right and left, but I do not recollect of any of our men being hit by them.

We could hear the enemy ahead of us, as we pressed our tired horses through the burning wagons and the scattered plunder which filled the road, giving our own wagon-rats and skulkers a fine harvest of plunder. Many of the wagons were untouched, but standing in the road without horses, the teamsters at the first alarm taking them out and making for the woods, coming back and taking their wagons again after the stampede was over, sometimes to find them plundered by our own cowardly skulkers, that I suppose belong to all armies. I have no doubt Cæsar had them in his tenth legion, and Xenophon in his famous ten thousand.

So far the enemy, in carrying out his plan of attack, had kept in motion; but after passing a large creek that crosses the road and runs on by "Amelia Springs," they halted at an old field on the side of the road and made a front. As the head of our column crossed the creek a lady was standing in the mud by the road side with a soldier in a "grey jacket." She had been with the ordnance train—the ambulance in which she had been riding was taken, the horses carried off, and as we closed up she was left as we found her. She was from Mississippi, and had left

Richmond with her friends in the "Artillery," and was much more mad than scared, and she stood there in the mud (she was young and pretty) and gesticulated as she told her story, making up a picture striking and peculiar. There was no time to listen, but promising to do our best to punish the aggressors, who had taken her up and dropped her so unceremoniously in the mud, which was the amount of the damage, and advising her to take shelter in a large white house on the hill, we moved on to meet the party ahead, who, near enough their reserve now for support, had halted to give us a taste of their quality.

At first they called out to come on and get their "greenbacks," seeing the small party in advance with the General, but as the regiments rode into the field, which was large enough to make a display of the entire line, they stood but to exchange a scattering fire, and then moved in retreat along a road running parallel to the main road and leading to "Amelia Springs." The Seventh, from position, was the leading regiment, and moved at a gallop in pursuit. The road swept round a point of wood on the left and an old field on the right grown up with pine. In advance rode five well mounted men of the regiment, as a lookout, led by the adjutant—General Gary immediately behind them—and the head of our column, the Seventh cavalry, next. As the advance guard rounded the bend in the road it was swept by the fire of the enemy, who had halted for that purpose, wheeling instantly in retreat as soon as they delivered their fire. Four men out of the five, all except the adjutant, were hit, one of them in the spine, "Mills," an approved scout, and one of the best and bravest men in the army. Throwing his arms over his head with a yell of agony, wrung from him by intense pain, he pitched backwards off his horse, which was going at full speed. The horse, a thoroughbred mare, kept on with us in the rush. (I will here say that I never saw the young man again—he was just in front of me when he fell—until three or four years after, in a pulpit, as a Presbyterian preacher. He had gotten over his wound without its doing him permanent injury). On we went, picking up some of the rear of the party who had not moved quick enough. The main body had gotten where there were thick woods on both sides of the road, where they halted to make a stand. But we were upon them before they made their wheel to face to the rear, or rather while they were in the act of making it, and so had them at advantage; we were among them with the sabre. The work was short and sharp, and we drove them along the road clear of the wood into the open field, where there was a strong dismounted reserve. Here we caught a fire that dropped two of our leading horses—Captain Caldwell's and Lieutenant Hinson's. Caldwell's horse was killed dead. Hinson's fell with a broken leg, catching his rider under him and holding him until relieved. A heavy fire swept the woods and road, so we dismounted the brigade as fast as the men came up, extending the dismounted line along the front of the enemy's fire, and moving to the left as he fell back to a stronger position. As we moved in advance they gave up the position by the house they had first taken, fell back across the field and ravine to the top of the opposite hill, where they halted in force and threw up temporary breastworks, made from a rail fence, and from that position repeated the invitation to "Come and get greenbacks." We moved up, occupied the ravine immediately in their front, which was deep enough to shelter the mounted officers, the line officers and the men being dismounted. Here General Gary determined to hold his position, until General Fitz Lee, who commanded our cavalry, came up, not deeming it advisable to attack the enemy in his present position and numbers. In half an hour's time General Fitz Lee came up with his division, dismounted his men, formed line, flanked the position, charged it in front, two or three heavy volleys, a shout and a rush. The enemy finding his position untenable moved off to the main body, not more than two or three miles from them—moving rapidly, as we found several of their wounded on the roadside, left in the hurry of their retreat. We moved on slowly after them—the sun being nearly down—to "Amelia Springs," some two miles off, crossed the creek, and, though we had commenced the fight in the morning, were politely requested (everybody knows what a military request is) by General Lee to move down the road until we could see the Yankee pickets, put the brigade into camp, post pickets, and make the best of it—all of which we did.

We did not have far to go to find the pickets—about a mile; posted our own two or three hundred yards from the brigade; sent to the mill on the creek at "Amelia Springs" and drew rations of flour and bacon.

I had here one of those unexpected surprises that sometimes gleam upon us under the most unpropitious circumstances. As we rode up to the big white house on the hill General Fitz Lee stood giving orders for the disposition of the troops. Our men were in numbers filling their canteens with water at the well in the yard, when a lieutenant from the Hampton Legion came from the well with his canteen in his hand. "B.," I said, "I am very thirsty; will you give me a drink from your canteen?" "Certainly, sir," said he, and handed it to me. I took a large swallow and discovered it was excellent old apple brandy. I had eaten nothing since a very light breakfast; had been working hard in the saddle all day; had the breath knocked out of my body by a spent ball on the chest at the close of the charge in the woods; the excitement of the fight was over, and I was lying over the pommel, rather than sitting on my saddle, but as that electric fluid went down my throat I straightened up like a soldier at the word of command; I felt a new life pouring through my veins, and the worry and care of the situation was all gone, and I was ready for what was to come next—such is the power of contrast. B., who was watching me, raised a warning finger not to betray his secret, for what was a canteen of apple brandy to that crowd, that would not be denied? so I concealed my satisfaction and his secret, but have never forgotten my obligation to Lieutenant B. of the Hampton Legion.

All around us through the stillness floated the music of the Yankee bands, mocking with their beautiful music our desperate condition; yet our men around their fires were enjoying it as much, and, seemingly, with as light hearts as the owners of it. Occasionally, as a bugle call would ring out, which always sounds to a trooper as a challenge to arms, a different expression would show itself, and a harder look take the place of the softer one induced by "Home, Sweet Home," or "Annie Lawrie."

So we made our bivouac in sight of the enemy's pickets, eating our homely rations with the keen relish and appetite health and hard work give. While our neighbors, whose interest in us could not be questioned, gave us the benefit of many a soft air, that told of other and very different scenes, we, in the language of romance, addressed ourselves to slumber, expecting an attack at or before daylight. This was our first night in sight of their outposts, and we had yet to learn their plan of attack. The game was in the toils and they meant to play a sure hand, with no more waste of material than was absolutely necessary. There was no night attack that I recollect in the course of the retreat. General Grant's large force seemed to be kept perfectly in hand, massed with great care to strike with effect at any given point on our line of march, gain the result of an overwhelming attack in force, and draw off in time to prevent disorder among their own troops—a wise arrangement under the circumstances.

Another pleasing incident occurred at this camp, as everything is relative and is great or little, according to circumstances. One of the non-commissioned officers of my old company came to me and asked if I would like to have my canteen filled with some very fine old apple brandy. One of General Lee's couriers had found a barrel of it covered up with leaves in an adjoining piece of woods, and let a few of his friends into the secret. Would I? Of course I would, and if we ever came out ahead I would recommend him for promotion. The canteen came full, and proved to be of the same tap as the "long swallow" was of which I had partaken so unexpectedly. That canteen of apple brandy, like Boniface's ale, was meat and drink for the rest of the time I was a soldier of the Southern Confederacy.

We got off about eight o'clock in the morning, not having been disturbed, as we expected, moved back across the creek that runs through the meadows at the foot of the hill below the hotel at "Amelia Springs," halted and formed line, facing to the rear along the creek, from the ford at the road down the creek to the mill, destroyed the bridge, and held the position as rear-guard, until General Lee, whose camp was above us on the hill, around the hotel, formed his column and moved, we following slowly in the rear.

We marched that day, until the afternoon, among the infantry, artillery and wagons, going towards Farmville, on the Appomattox river and the Lynchburg railroad. There was a bridge across the river, at which, as was afterwards shown, it was General Lee's purpose to cross his infantry wagons and artillery.

We had been having a very tiresome march on our worn-out horses, through the fields on the side of the road, giving up the road proper to the wagon trains and troops, sometimes dismounting and leading our horses, to relieve them as much as possible.

About two or three o'clock we saw the infantry in front of us breaking from the line of march by brigades into a large field on the left of the road, and rapidly forming into compact masses in proper position and relation with one another, to be used as might be required. We halted and did the same, being the only cavalry at that point. We soon heard heavy firing on another road over to the right, two or three miles from us, artillery and small arms, and nearer to us—not a mile—was a lesser fight going on, to which we moved at once. The last, which was over before we got to it, was between General Lee's division of cavalry and a body of the enemy's infantry. They were, as we were told, a fresh set of troops who had just come on, and were literally gobbled up by Lee. We met the prisoners—some eight or nine hundred—going to the rear. Their coats were so new and blue, and buttons so bright, and shirts so clean, that it was a wonder to look upon them by our rusty lot.

They were pushing on to coöperate with the larger movement that was going on to the right, and fell in with General Lee's cavalry, and after a very respectable fight had their military experience brought to an abrupt conclusion. Lee's men had possessed themselves of a complete set of new brass instruments that formed their band.

The fight on the right was the heaviest and most damaging to us that occurred on the retreat, and is known as the Battle of "Sailor's Creek," or "High Bridge," where the divisions of General Kershaw and General Custis Lee, under the command of Lieutenant General Ewell, were knocked to pieces—and General Richard Anderson's command, composed of Pickett's Division and Bushrod Johnson's, with Huger's artillery. Pickett's and Huger's commands were, I think, destroyed, but Johnson managed to get through. Generals Kershaw, Ewell and Lee were, I know, taken prisoners. All this we knew nothing of at the time, only that there was heavy fighting, and that being a matter of course, excited no surprise.

The sun was nearly down and we moved towards Farmville, to go into camp for the night. It was after dark when we got there, went through the town to the grove on the other side, and made the best of it. We lived upon what we could pick up, as we had no wagons with us, and our servants and spare horses were with the wagon train.

The most fruitful source of supply was when we passed a broken down commissary wagon. The men would fill their haversacks with whatever they could find; and whatever they got, either in this way or at the country houses, was liberally shared with their friends and officers.

By a big fire we lay down, and slept the sleep of the tired. The nights were cold, so near the mountains, and, with light coverings on the cold ground, the burning down of the fire was a general awakening and building up of the same. At one of these movements we were surprised to find, between Colonel H. and myself, two men, who, attracted by the fire, cold and tired, had crept to its friendly warmth, making a needless apology for their presence. We found one to be a colonel of Pickett's division, the other a lieutenant, and realized fully how complete the destruction of that famous fighting division must have been as an organization, that we should find a regimental commander who did not know where to look for its standard. There seemed to be no particular hurry in getting off in the morning. We were waiting for orders by our fire, and filled up the time pressing horses in the town, from a kind consideration of the feelings of the owners, that they should not fall into the hands of the Yankees, much to the disgust of the said owners, who seemed much to prefer (good men and true as they were) the possible chance of the Yankee to the certainty of the Confederate abstraction.

One or two amusing incidents occurred in that connection. One of our young lieutenants had heard of a very fine bay stallion, belonging to a gentleman in town, and as the rumor had spread that pressing horse flesh was going on, he went off promptly with a man or two, reached the house, and was met at the door by a young and pretty woman, who, with all the elegant kindness of a Virginia lady, asked him to come in. He felt doubtful, but could not resist; ordering his men to hold on a minute or two, while he talked horse with the lady, wishing, in the innocent kindness of his heart, to break it to her gently. After a few minutes' general conversation he touched on the horse question. "Oh! yes, sir," she said, getting up and looking through a window that overlooked the back yard. "Yes, sir; I am sorry to disappoint you, but as you came in at the front door my husband was saddling the bay, and while you were talking to me I saw him riding out of the back gate. I am so sorry; indeed I am." With a hasty good morning our lieutenant rode back to camp upon a horse some degrees below the standard of a "Red Eye" or any other race horse. The laugh was with the lady.

Another case was against a class who met with but little sympathy from a soldier in the field—a local or collecting quartermaster, when of a particular class—some able bodied young man, every way fit for the soldier, except in spirit, getting the position to screen himself from field duty and make money out of a suffering people. The order had been given through the brigade to take the horses wherever they could be found. A wagon with two good horses drove between our fire and that of the squadron lying next. A captain stepped out, stopped the wagon, and the horses were taken out and appropriated—the boy driving them ran off—and soon there came riding up a dashing young quartermaster on a fine grey horse, groomed to perfection, and horse and rider redolent of the sybaritism of the department, claimed the horses as belonging to his department, with a most insolent air, looking daggers and court martials, and swelling as only overfed subsistence agents on home duty could do. While he was talking I saw Captain D. walking round him looking at the gallant grey, and then at our colonel inquiringly. A nod from the colonel and Captain D's hand was on the grey's bridle, and a quiet but firm request, that sounded very much like an order, for him to get down, as his horse was wanted for cavalry service. The man of the subsistence and transportation department was so dumbfounded that he would have let pass the best operation possible of making money out of the necessities of the people for which his tribe was famous; but just then a bugle rang out the call for "boot and saddle;" the bugles of the other regiments took it up; the momentary diversion of the horse pressing and the quartermaster was forgotten; work was at hand; the rumbling of the artillery and wagons crossing the bridge, with columns of infantry between, could be heard down in the town at the foot of the hill, and the cavalry were wanted on the other side of the town, by the Randolph House, to hold the enemy in check and cover the crossing of the river.

The brigade was soon in the saddle, and moving at a swinging trot down the long street that constitutes mainly the town of Farmville. As the regiment passed a large building on the right, which was shown to be a boarding school for young ladies, from the number gathered on the piazza in front, we were greeted by their waving handkerchiefs and moist eyes, while cheer after cheer rose from our men in response to their kindness and sympathy. They did not know, as we did, that their friends and defenders were to pass by, leaving them so soon in the hands most dreaded by them. They saw us going to the front; our men were excited by the circumstances and the prospect of a fight, and the light of that wild glory that belongs to war shone over it all. The rough, grey soldier, the tramping column, and the groups of tender girls, mixed with it like flowers on a battle field, incongruous in detail, but blending with the picture, like discords in music, making it complete.

So on through the town, across the little stream, and up the hill, on the top of which on the right stood a large white building, called, as I recollect, the Randolph House; in the field around were gathered and gathering large bodies of our cavalry, under the command of General F.H. Lee, General Rosser and other distinguished cavalry officers. We took our position among them. As before stated, our column, artillery and wagon train, were pouring in a steady stream across the bridge, and the enemy were pressing up their artillery, and already throwing long shots at it from batteries not near enough to do much if any harm, and too much under cover to admit of an effectual attack from us.

General Lee dismounted the most of his command and formed a line of battle along the road looking toward the point from which the enemy were advancing.

We (our brigade) were kept in the saddle at the point we first occupied on the right of the road. There was a house some three hundred yards from the road on the left, directly in front of General Lee's line, in a grove of oak, with a lane or avenue leading to it from the main road. Behind the house a battery seemed gradually advancing and already throwing its shells at or about the bridge. So far they were completely masked by the house, and we could only judge of their movements from their fire, which seemed closer every moment.

In pursuance of some order we changed our position, and rode to General Lee's dismounted line of battle. As we rode up—our regiment, the Seventh, leading—we were the right flank regiment in the brigade formation, and in column with the right in front were necessarily in advance. The battery seemed by this time to have gotten immediately behind the house, and was pitching shells about the bridge and into the town (the bridge was at the foot of the street) with precision and rapidity. Expecting to see it unmask itself in front of the house every moment, General Lee said to our colonel, "Haskell, as soon as that battery shows itself take it with your regiment; you can do it."

31

We moved at once down the avenue toward the house up to the edge of the oak wood, with which the lawn in front was surrounded, formed the regiment in column of fours in the road. The colonel rode along the side of the column, the adjutant detailing three of the best mounted men from each company—the horses were the animals specially selected—the men at that stage of the game were all known to be good—making thirty men, and the senior captain, Doby, in immediate command of the party.

The colonel rode in front of the halted column some forty or fifty yards, with his thirty men, after directing the officer next in command to ride down the flank of the regiment, form, and speak to each "set of fours" separately. Each set of fours waited for the word of command to be given to themselves specially, and as the order was given "to close up and dress," they did so steadily and firmly, and I looked into the eyes of each man in the regiment, and they looked into mine. There was little left for words to say.

There we sat, waiting to charge the battery that was momentarily expected to unmask in front of the house—something over two hundred men of the thousand on our muster roll, and all the cavalry of the army of Northern Virginia, looking on to see how we did it.

The shells from the battery whistled four or five feet above our heads, for they had discovered our line on the hill and turned their fire on it. The shells went over our heads, but struck a few feet in front of General Lee's dismounted line, making gaps in it as they did so.

Just then information was received that our marching column had crossed the bridge—our charge was not to be—there was nothing to wait for. General Lee mounted his men, formed, and moved off promptly to cross the river at a ford some two miles farther up, leaving General Gary with his brigade to cover his retreat. We drew off from the position we had taken to attack the battery, the regiment resuming its position at the head of the brigade, with the exception of Colonel Haskell, Captain Doby, and the thirty men before chosen—this party remained in the rear of the brigade, all moving off slowly, the last of General Lee's division having by this time gone out of sight over the top of the hill.

We had not yet been able to perceive that the bridge was on fire. General Gary said that General Lee had left it to his discretion to cross at the bridge if he could, as he expected we would be pressed very closely at the last; so, instead of following General Lee's line of retreat, we turned down towards the town again and halted in the street while the General himself galloped down to the bridge to see if it was practicable. The shells were bursting over the town, and in the street occasionally, while the good people of Farmville, in a state of great though natural alarm, were leaving with their goods forthwith. We told them we were going at once; were not to make a fight in the town; to keep quiet in their houses, and it was not probable they would be interfered with.

The bridge, bursting into smoke and flame, told the story before the General got back. On we went up the street, through the grove where we camped the night before, on toward the railroad, following the track taken by General Lee.

Just beyond the wood, on the outskirts of the town, a large creek runs under the railroad through an arched way or viaduct, wide enough for the road to pass along its bank. After crossing this creek, on a bridge on the town side of the railroad embankment, we passed along the road under the culvert, and formed on the edge of the woods some three or four hundred yards beyond. Colonel Haskell, with Captain Doby and his thirty men, halted at the bridge to destroy it, as by this time bodies of the enemy's cavalry could be seen moving at a gallop on the hill above. The creek was too deep for a ford; so it was all important, in connection with our crossing the river, to check their advance by burning the bridge. Colonel Haskell, dismounting, placed all of his party, except his axemen, behind the railroad bank which overlooked the bridge and served as a capital breastwork, went to work with a will. By this time the enemy was upon them and commenced a heavy fire, which was returned handsomely by the party under cover and with good effect. Colonel Haskell succeeded in the complete destruction of the bridge, with the loss of only one of his axemen killed.

The cover of the bank, and the small number actually exposed when at work, enabled him to perform a gallant and dangerous piece of service with slight loss.

General Gary, who had occupied a position between the wood where the brigade was formed and near where the bridge party was at work, so as to be in complete command of whatever might take place, moved on at once toward the ford where General Lee had already crossed his division. We moved by regiments in intervals after him.

By some mistake of our guide we were carried to a point in the river which was not practicable, at the then stage of the river, as a ford—which we duly discovered after nearly drowning two or three men and horses of the ambulance train, whom we found at the head of the column when we reached the river, their usual place being in the rear. The adjutant, finding them in front, asked them, "What the deuce are you doing here—your place is in the rear?" "No, sir," said a long-backed individual of the party, in a copper colored raiment, who seemed to have been making a study of the rules and regulations as applying to his own department. "Not so. In the rear, I grant you, in the advance; in the front, if you please, in a retreat" "So be it," said I. "In with you;" and in they went, nothing loth. The river was swimming and the horses swam badly, making plunges to reach the opposite bank, which, when they gained, was steep and treacherous, and it was only after repeated efforts, and their riders getting off into the river, that they made a landing. It was apparent that this could not be the point that General Lee had crossed his division. Some one turned up who led us right. About a mile farther up we found the ford that he had crossed at, and got over without difficulty or molestation; it was scarcely swimming to the smallest horse, and directly opposite lay all of the Virginia cavalry to cover our crossing, if pressed, while it was going on. We were the first regiment that crossed; found some stacks of oats; halted, formed in squadrons, fed our horses, ate what we had to eat, rested, and, as usual, made the best of it.

After a rest of about an hour General Lee moved off, we following in his rear, the Virginians ahead of us with General Lee destroying the equanimity of the good people on their line of march by pressing every horse found in their way. It seemed hard to come down so on our own people, after all the sacrifices already made by them, but if the horse was lost by our taking him, which was apt to be the result, the proceeding mounted at least one of our own troopers; on the other hand it gave a fresh horse to the enemy, and was equally lost to the owner—and this was the view the Virginians usually took of it. General Lee, being ahead of us, made a clean sweep as he went along, leaving scarce a gleaning of horseflesh for us. After a while we came upon the wagons and infantry again. It was not long before the ringing of a volley and the roar of a piece of artillery let us know that an attack had been made on our train again. We moved up to the firing at a gallop, and as we passed along there came sweeping through the woods, from the road running parallel with the one we were on, a body of infantry in line, moving at a double quick upon the same point, which was but a short distance ahead of us. They were what was left of the famous "Texas brigade," well remembered by some of us in 1861 on the Occoquon at Dumfries—first commanded by Wigfall, then a short time by Archer, then by Hood, then Gregg, who was killed October 26th, 1864, at the fight on the Darbytown road. At this time the brigade counted about one hundred and thirty muskets, commanded by Colonel Duke. We had been fighting with them all summer, from Deep Bottom to New Market heights, to the lines around Richmond, and they recognized the brigade as we rode along their front, and with a yell as fierce and keen as when their three regiments averaged a thousand strong, and nothing but victory had been around their flag, they shouted to us, "Forward, boys, forward, and tell them Texas is coming!"

When we got into the open field we found that General Lee's division of cavalry had engaged the enemy, driven him from his attack on our train, and taken the Federal General Gregg prisoner.

The enemy were occupying in force, apparently, the woods on the light of the field with infantry and artillery. We were holding the open field which had been the scene of the skirmish before we came up, and threw out skirmishers, and returned the fire of their sharpshooters—both sides using a piece or two of artillery at long range.

After this had gone on for a while, "ours," the Seventh, was ordered to charge in line on horseback, through a piece of old field, grown up in scattering pines, upon the battery that was working on us from the edge of the oak woods. The line was formed and we went at it very handsomely, our men keeping up their line and fire astonishingly, considering we were armed with "muzzle loaders" (the greatest possible of all drawbacks to the efficiency of cavalry).

We drew on ourselves at once a heavy fire of artillery and small arms, which told smartly on our line, knocking over men and horses, until the left flank of the regiment came upon a ravine, or deep wash, covering nearly half of its front. The horses could not cross. We moved by the right flank to clear the obstruction, and then found that the object of our demonstration had been answered. It had been made to cover the withdrawal of a body of our infantry that had been advanced on our right. It was sundown. We left a strong line of pickets, or rather a skirmish line, under command of Lieutenant Munerlyn, upon the ground we had occupied, and drew off into the open field, waiting for dark before going into camp, or rather lying on our arms. It had been a tiresome day, and, though neither then nor now an admirer of strong drink, I fell back upon and fully appreciated the contents of my canteen—the famous apple brandy of Amelia Springs.

This, although we did not know it then, was destined to be (save the last of all) the hardest night upon us. We moved into a piece of woods as soon as it was dark, and formed the regiment in squadrons, with orders to water horses, a squadron at a time—the rest holding position, the men in the saddle, until the return of the preceding squadron—and then picket their horses and make fires as near as possible on the same ground. But when the first squadron returned from the water, and the field officers had just unbuckled their sabres and stretched themselves on the ground to take the rest so much needed, and watch that most interesting process to a hungry man, the building up the little fire that was to do his modest cooking, when an orderly comes from General Gary to change camp—to buckle up and mount, and follow the orderly a half mile to the rear. We were, it seemed, too near the enemy's line, looking to the contemplated movement.

At the new location—a comfortable piece of piny woods old field—we finished what we had begun at the other point. At our mess, sleep seemed to be the great object in view. I went to sleep immediately, my head on my saddle; woke in about a half hour's time to eat what there was, and instantly to sleep again; but that was not to be. At about ten o'clock a quiet order mounted us, almost before, as the little boys say, we got the "sleep out of our eyes." We were in column on the road, and non-commissioned officers under the direction of the adjutant riding down it, each with a handkerchief full of cartridges, supplying the men with that very necessary "article of war." And then commenced that most weary night march, that will always be remembered by the tired men who rode it, that ended only (without a halt, except a marching one,) at Appomattox Court-house.

The line of retreat had been changed, and by a forced night march on another road a push was being made for the mountains at Lynchburg. Had we gotten there (and Appomattox Court-house was within twenty miles of Lynchburg) with the men and material General Lee still had with him, Lee's last struggle among the mountains of his native State would have made a picture to swell the soldier's heart with pride to look upon. The end we know would have been the same; a few more noble hearts would have bled in vain, and song and story would but have found new themes to tell the old, old tale—how willing brave men are to die for what they believe to be right. Through long lines of toiling wagons, artillery trains and tired men, we pushed on as rapidly as we could; at a bad piece of road, at a creek or a muddy hill, the column sometimes got cut in two by a portion getting through the wagons, the train then closing, waiting upon a wagon mired down ahead.

At one of these halts for the brigade to close up and for the regiments to report position, General Gary had halted at a large fire made from the rails of some good farmer's fence by troops ahead of us, and round it we all gathered, for the night was cold. The subject of conversation with the brigade staff when we joined was, that Captain M., the inspector, not being well, had, early in the night, halted at a farm house and gone to bed, just to see how it would feel, putting his horse in the farmer's stable; and when he roused himself to the necessities of his position, and sought to ride with the rest, he found his horse was gone. Some pressing party had gone that way.

I remembered, when I listened to the drowsy talk about the captain's loss, that a couple of enterprising young fellows had reported some horses at a farm house and gotten permission to go after them. They had not long returned with their prizes; they, the horses, stood just on the edge of light thrown by the fire against the darkness that rose like a wall behind it, the hind-quarters of one, a large, leggy bay, with stockings on his hind legs, could be seen from where we sat; one of the orderlies,

37

looking with sleepy eyes from the log on which he was sitting at the horses, expressed himself to the effect that he thought that "long-legged bay" looked about the hind-quarters a good deal like the captain's missing charger. And so it proved. While the captain "dallied at Capua," pressing the luxurious blanket of the Virginia farmer, his horse, in camp parlance, was "lifted" by our enterprising youth; and, much to their disgust, the captain reëntered into possession of his leggy war horse. They expressed themselves to the effect that they would as soon have stolen his horse as any body else's.

Again in the saddle, tramping through mud holes, splashing in ruts, we worked our way amid the long line of wagons, troops and artillery, until daylight came to our relief. About eight o'clock we came upon our own wagon train—the first, and, by the way, the only time we encountered it on our route—comfortably camped in a fine grove, good fires, and a glorious smell of cooking permeating the early morning air. The headquarter wagons of our regiment were parked near a fine fire, and our servants (never expecting to see us again, I suppose,) were cooking on a large scale from our private stores for a half dozen notorious wagon-rats of the genteeler sort.

Of course, as we rode up our boys declared they expected us and were getting breakfast ready, which statement was sustained by "messieurs," the wagon-rats; but the longing look they cast at a big pot of rice steaming by the fire as they drew off, indicated a deeper interest than I think it possible for them to have gotten up on any one's account but their own. We had a most comfortable breakfast and a rest of an hour only, the time being taken up in dozing and eating.

Bad as the night had been the day was a beautiful one. The sun was shining bright; our breakfast and rest had so refreshed us, short as that rest was, that we resumed our march and the work before us, cheerful and ready to meet it, whatever it might be, and what that "might be" was no man troubled himself to know.

Not long after resuming our march we posted pickets at some cross roads, under the immediate direction of General R.E. Lee himself. We moved steadily on to-day without molestation of any kind, the wagons moving in double lines, the road being wide enough to admit it. About twelve o'clock or a little later we had halted to water our horses at a stream that crossed the road. It takes a good deal of time for a large body of cavalry to water their horses, particularly if the stream is small, and the men have to be watched closely to prevent their fouling the water.

I had dismounted and was leaning across my horse, when I saw, as I thought, Captain Allen, of the Twenty-fourth Virginia, of our brigade, having watered his horse where the stream crossed the road. The captain was a fine specimen of a Virginia soldier and gentleman, some sixty years of age, of fine presence, who was always said to resemble General Lee, wearing his grey beard trimmed after the fashion of that of our great leader, and in the saddle having about the same height, though dismounted, the captain, I should say, was the taller. However, I watched the old captain, as I thought, riding up the hill toward me, on a very fine grey horse, and was thinking what a type of the veteran soldier he looked, as indeed I had often thought before, until he got within a few feet of me, when I changed my intended rather familiar, but still most respectful salute, meant for the captain, for the reverence with which the soldier salutes the standard of his legion—which represents to him all that he has left to love and honor—as I discovered that it was General R.E. Lee himself, riding alone—not even an orderly in attendance. He returned our salute, his eye taking it all in, with a calm smile, that assured us our confidence was not misplaced. He bore the pressure of the responsibility that was upon him as only a great and good man could— as one who felt that, happen what may, selfishness—consideration of what might happen to himself—had nothing to do with it.

So I felt satisfied that there was a likeness between Captain Allen, of the Twenty-fourth Virginia, and General R.E. Lee of the Southern Confederacy.

A little after this we got orders to move on, as quickly as we could, in advance to Appomattox Court-house. "Appomattox Court-house" is a small county town about a mile from the Lynchburg railroad. At the foot of the hill on which the courthouse and the three or four houses that constitute the village stand, run the headwaters of the Appomattox river, a small stream, not knee deep to a horse.

As soon as we cleared the wagon train we got over ground much faster, and rode into and through the town just as the sun was setting. We stopped at a piece of woods on the outskirts of the village, and halted in the road while the quartermasters were selecting the ground, and the regiments were closing up. Our foragers, that had been detailed before we got into town, were riding in with the hay they had collected on the pommels of their saddles, and all was as quiet as a scene in "Arcady," when the stillness was broken by the scream of a shell, the report of a gun, and then the burst-up of the missile as it finished its mission and reported progress—and then another, and another, until as pretty battery practice was developed down yonder by the depot—Clover Hill I think it is called—as you would wish to hear.

Without knowing positively anything about it, those whom I had conversed with relative to our pushing on to the Court house were under the impression that a large body of our infantry were ahead of us— General Dick Anderson's corps. He was there, as it turned out, but his corps had been expended a day or two before; it had been completely fought out, for we had no better officer than Lt. General Richard Anderson, an old West Pointer—cavalry at that—and a South Carolinian to boot.

It was, however, "hammer and tongs" down there at all events—shell, grape and canister at short range. Custar's division of Sheridan's cavalry had taken the chord of the arc, and reached the depot just about the time we got to the village. A knowledge of his movements had caused our being sent forward, his object being to strike the artillery train, which was in advance of us—sixty pieces, under General Walker. Three batteries were left at the depot to hold it, while the rest retreated along the Lynchburg pike. The three batteries were six guns under command of Major James C. Coit—consisting of two guns Pegram's battery, Va., Lieut. Scott; two guns Wright's battery, Va., Lieut. Atkisson; two guns Martin's battery, Va., Capt. Martin; with sixteen men, Kelly's battery, S.C., Lieut. Race, who assisted in working Wright's guns.

While we were closing up our scattered ranks, and getting the brigade ready for action as rapidly as coolness, skill and courage could do it, a department officer (I think he was) came galloping up to us from the scene of action, apparently under orders from himself to get out of the way; but the natural insolence of his class broke out in spite of the scare that was on him, and he commenced giving orders at once. I happened to be the person addressed—"Get on at once; the enemy are down yonder Why don't you go at once? Are all you men going to stand here and let the enemy"—and so on. The colonel had ridden down the column to see that all was straight, while the "Legion" and the Twenty-fourth Virginia were closing up, so that when we did move it would be as a compact body—when the order came ringing along—"Forward, forward, men! gallop!"—and our indignant friend was lost in the rush of the column while yet haranguing us for being so slow.

The roar of the batteries was incessant. They were evidently holding the dismounted cavalry in check. As rapidly as we could get over ground we moved towards them, and formed the brigade in the field to the left of the position held by the batteries, in what might be called a column of regiments. As we formed the regiment from a column of fours into line, they came down from a gallop to a trot at the order, "Front into line," as steadily as if on parade; then followed, "Right dress, front"—and all were ready for the next move.

Our batteries from the right were shelling the woods opposite to us. In front, under cover, some of the cavalry skirmishers were using their Spencers upon us at long range, and a squadron of ours, the Fifth, was detailed to move up and take a position opposite and return their fire.

By this time the grey of twilight was lighted up by the rising moon, and there seemed to be a lull in the attack. General Gary and Colonel Haskell had ridden over our front and communicated with the commanding officer of the batteries; the consequence of which was, the brigade was dismounted and double-quicked through a small piece of wood to the batteries. Before our men could get to the guns the enemy charged and got among them, but were driven back by the fire and our rush, but taking with them some of our men as prisoners—among them Captain Hankins, of the Virginia battery, who got away and came running up to me as I rode to my place. Our men fell in between the guns, and then began one of the closest artillery fights, for the numbers engaged and the time it lasted, that occurred during the war. The guns were fought literally up to the muzzles. It was dark by this time, and at every discharge the cannon was ablaze from touch-hole to mouth, and there must have been six or eight pieces at work, and the small arms of some three or four hundred men packed in among the guns in a very confined space. It seemed like the very jaws of the lower regions. They made three distinct charges, preluding always with the bugle, on the right, left and centre, confusing the point of attack; then, with a cheer and up they came. It was too dark to see anything under the shadow of the trees but the long dark line. They would get within thirty or forty yards of the guns and then roll back, under the deadly fire that was poured upon them from the artillery and small arms. Amid the flashing, and the roaring, and the shouting, rose the wild yell of a railroad whistle, as a train rushed up almost among us (the enemy had possession of the road), as we were fighting around the depot, sounding on the night air as if the devil himself, had just come up and was about to join in what was going on.

Then came a lull; our friends in front seemed to have had the wire edge taken off.

Our horses had been sent back to the turnpike road; General Gary taking advantage of the present quiet sent Colonel Haskell to get them together—rather a difficult task, as it afterwards proved.

General Gary's great object was to draw off the guns, if possible, now night had set in, from the depot, and get them back with the rest of the train in the line of retreat. So the order was given to limber them up, which was done, and the guns moved off at once, it being but a few hundred yards to the main road.

Our brigade in line faced to the rear, the guns behind them, and covered the movement. The silence of the guns soon told our friends over yonder what was going on, and they were not long in following after; our men, facing to the rear, delivered their fire steadily, moving in retreat, facing and firing every few steps, effectually keeping off a rush; they pressed us, but cautiously—the darkness concealed our numbers.

We were going through an open old field, and came now to a road through a narrow piece of woods, where we broke from line into column, and double-quicked through the woods so as to get to the road beyond. Before we got to the turnpike we heard the bugles of the enemy down it, and as the head of our column came into the road their cavalry charged the train some two or three hundred yards below us. Sixty pieces of cannon, at the point where we came into the road, the drivers were attempting to turn back toward the Court House, had got entangled with one another and presented a scene of utter confusion.

As our regiment got into the road some thirty or forty men were thrown out from the last squadron and faced to the rear on the right and left, opening a fire directly upon those of the dismounted men who were pressing us from that quarter. I had but little fear of the enemy's cavalry riding into us on the road, so blocked up as it was with the routed artillery train, and there were woods on both sides just here.

In passing from the old field, where the guns had been at work, into the woods that separated it from the turnpike, two men were walking just in front of me, following their gun, which was on before. I heard one say, "Tout perdu." I asked at once, "What battery do you belong to?" "Donaldsonville." It was the creole company; and they might well have added the other words of the great Francis, after the battle of Pavia, "Tout perdu fors l'honneur" all lost but honor; for well had they done their work from 'sixty-one, when they came to Virginia, until now, when all was lost, "Tout perdu"—it was the motto of the occasion.

The stag was in the toils, but the end was not yet. We could hear the rush, the shouts and pistol shots, where the enemy mounted and in force had attacked the train; the artillerymen having no arms could make no fight, as they could not use their pieces. We could do nothing (being closely pressed by a superior force of their dismounted men) but fall back upon the town toward our main body, making the best front we could, leaving the road and marching under cover of the timber on the side, being on foot giving us a better position to resist any attack that might be made upon us by the cavalry.

The fifth squadron of the Seventh, that had been thrown out as skirmishers when we first came on the ground, had kept their position covering our left flank when the fight at the batteries was going on. And when we commenced falling back after the guns, the adjutant, Lieutenant Capers, was sent to bring them to the road, so as to join the regiment. They had also been dismounted, and their horses sent with the rest. He found them, led them to the road, and, on getting on it at a point nearer to the town than where we struck it, hearing the bugles and the rush of the cavalry on the train, he at once posted the companies, with their captains, Doby and Dubose, in the woods immediately on the road-side, and with the parting salutation, "Take care of yourselves, boys," (he had been a private in one of the companies, and both were from his native district), dashed back to his place in the regiment and disappeared round a turn in the road. They had scarcely lost sight of him when a heavy volley rang out, and his horse came round the bend at full speed without his rider, jumping over in his fright a broken caisson that lay across the road—the horse, a very fine roan, the one he was riding when, at "Amelia Spring," he, Capers, was the only one of the five in advance who escaped, to meet his fate that night, pierced by a dozen balls; the whole fire of the column was concentrated upon him, for we found his body next day. Some kind hand had given him a soldier's grave; some one, most likely of those who fought us, who could not but respect and admire the gallant young fellow lying in his blood, and with the feeling developed by a soldier's life, "So be it to me and mine in my sorrow as I may be to thee this day." All the respect was shown that circumstances admitted of.

One of our captains, who was wounded at the "guns" severely, fell into the enemy's hands when we moved them—as everybody was too busy to look after the wounded, and ambulance men and stretchers were this time neither in the front or rear. He was taken up by his new friends quite tenderly, as he thought, and put into an ambulance; but in the course of the evening's entertainment the Yankee wounded came dropping in, and our friend, Captain Walker, was disposed of rather unceremoniously on the roadside, for others they valued at a higher rate than even a Confederate captain.

Immediately after the adjutant's horse came Custar's cavalry. Seeing all clear before them, they came on without a check until, when nearly opposite where our men of the Fifth squadron were lying in the woods, they caught the fire of the entire squadron, which emptied a good many saddles, and was the last shot probably fired that night.

The Federal cavalry kept on toward the town, and the squadron, under cover, drew deeper into the woods, and moved round the town and went into camp, but did not join the main body until next morning. The enemy

Photo Eng. Co. N.Y.

kept on until they got into, or nearly into the town, but again fell back, establishing their line somewhere between the town and the depot. Our outside picket was in the town.

We went into camp about one o'clock in the morning, on the Richmond side of the town, in the woods—General Gary riding to General Gordon's headquarters to report before lying down.

April 9th.—The sun rose clear on this the last day, practically, of the Southern Confederacy. It was cool and fresh in the early morning so near the mountains, though the spring must have been a forward one, as the oak trees were covered with their long yellow tassels.

We gathered the brigade on the green on the Richmond side of the village, most of the men on foot, the horses not having come in. About eight o'clock a large portion of our regiment had their horses—they having been completely cut off the night before by the charge of Custar's cavalry on the turnpike, and were carried, to save them, into a country cross-road. Then the "Hampton Legion" got theirs. My impression is that the Twenty-fourth Virginia lost the most or a good many of their horses. The men built fires, and all seemed to have something to eat, and to be amusing themselves eating it. The woods on the southern and eastern side swarmed with the enemy and their cavalry—a portion of it was between us and the "James River," which was about twelve miles distant. General Fitz Lee's division of cavalry lay over in that direction somewhere; General Longstreet with General Gordon was in and on the outer edge of the town, on the Lynchburg side, and so we waited for the performance to commence.

Looking at and listening to the men you would not have thought there was anything special in the situation. They turned all the responsibility over to the officers, who in turn did the same to those above them—the captain to the colonel, the colonel to the brigadier, and so on.

Colonel Haskell had not yet returned—having sent in all the horses he had gotten, and was still after the balance. About nine or ten o'clock, artillery firing began in front of General Longstreet, and the blue jackets showed in heavy masses on the edge of the woods. General Gary riding up, put everything that had a horse in the saddle, and moved us down the hill, just on the edge of the little creek that is here the "Appomattox," to wait under cover until wanted. Two of our young men, who had some flour and a piece of bacon in their haversacks, had improvised a cooking utensil out of a bursted canteen, and fried some cakes. They offered me a share in their meal, of which I partook with great relish. I then lay down, with my head, like the luxurious Highlander, upon a smooth stone, and, holding my horse's bridle in my hand, was soon in the deep sleep of a tired man. But not for long, for down came the general in his most emphatic manner—and those who know Gary know a man whose emphasis can be wonderfully strong when so minded. "Mount, men, mount!" I jumped up at the sharp, ringing summons with the sleep still in my eyes, and found myself manœuvring my horse with his rear in front. We soon had everything in its right place, and rode out from the bottom into the open field, about two hundred and fifty strong, to see the last of it.

Firing was going on, artillery and small arms, beyond the town, and there was General R.E. Lee himself, with Longstreet, Gordon, and the rest of his paladins.

When we rode into the open field we could see the enemy crowding along the edge of the woods—cavalry apparently extending their line around us. We kept on advancing towards them to get a nearer view of things, and were midway on the Richmond side between the town and a large white house with a handsome grove around it. In the yard could be seen a body of cavalry, in number about our own; we saw no other troops near. Two or three hundred yards to the right of the house an officer, apparently of rank, with a few men—his staff, probably—riding well forward, halted, looking toward the town with his glass. Just as he rode out General Gary had given the order to charge the party in the yard. Some one remarked that it looked like a flag of truce. "Charge!" swore Gary in his roughest tones, and on we went. The party in the yard were taken by surprise; they had not expected us to charge them, as they were aware that a parley was going on (of which, of course, we knew nothing), and that there was a suspension of hostilities.

We drove them through the yard, taking one or two prisoners—one little fellow, who took it very good-humoredly; he had his head tied up, having got it broken somewhere on the road, and was riding a mule. We followed up their retreat through the yard, down a road, through the open woods beyond, and were having it, as we thought, all our own way—when, stretched along behind the brown oaks, and moving with a close and steady tramp, was a long line of cavalry, some thousands strong—Custar's division—our friends of last night. This altered the complexion of things entirely; the order was instantly given to move by the left flank—which, without throwing our back to them, changed the forward into a retrograde movement.

The enemy kept his line unbroken, pressing slowly forward, firing no volley, but dropping shots from a line of scattered skirmishers in front was all we got They, of course, knew the condition of things, and seemed to think we did not. We fell back toward a battery of ours that was behind us, supported, I think, by a brigade of North Carolina infantry. We moved slowly, and the enemy's skirmishers got close enough for a dash to be made by our acting regimental adjutant—in place of Lieutenant Capers, killed the night before—Lieutenant Haile, who took a prisoner, but just as it was done one of our couriers—Tribble, Seventh regiment—mounted on a fine black horse, bareheaded, dashed between the two lines with a handkerchief tied upon a switch, sent by General Gordon, announcing the "suspension of hostilities."

By this time the enterprising adjutant had in turn been made prisoner. As soon as the orders were understood everything came to a stand-still, and for a while I thought we were going to have, then and there, a little inside fight on purely personal grounds.

An officer—a captain—I presume the captain in command of the party in the yard that we had attacked and driven back upon the main body—had, I rather expect, been laughed at by his own people for his prompt and sudden return from the expedition he had set out on.

He rode up at once to General Gary, and with a good deal of heat (he had his drawn sabre in his hand) wanted to know what he, Gary, meant by keeping up the fight after there had been a surrender. "Surrender!" said Gary, "I have heard of no surrender. We are South Carolinians, and don't surrender. [Ah! General, but we did, though.] Besides, sir, I take commands from no officers but my own, and I do not recognize you or any of your cloth as such."

The rejoinder was about to be a harsh one, sabres were out and trouble was very near, when an officer of General Custar's staff—I should like to have gotten his name—his manner was in striking contrast to that of the bellicose captain, who seemed rather to belong to the snorting persuasion—he, with the language and manner of a thorough gentleman, said, "I assure you, General, and I appreciate your feelings in the matter, that there has been a suspension of hostilities, pending negotiations, and General Lee and General Grant are in conference on the matter at this time."

His manner had its effect on General Gary, who at once sheathed his sabre, saying, "Do not suppose, sir, I have any doubt of the truth of your statement, but you must allow that, under such circumstances, I can only receive orders from my own officers; but I am perfectly willing to accept your statement and wait for those orders." (Situated as we were, certainly a wise conclusion.) Almost on the instant Colonel Blackford, of the engineers, rode up, sent by General Gordon, with a Federal officer, carrying orders to that effect.

48

We drew back to the artillery and infantry that were just behind us, and formed our battered fragments into regiments.

Desperate as we knew our condition to be since last night's affair, still the idea of a complete surrender, which we began now to see was inevitable, came as an awful shock. Men came to their officers with tears streaming from their eyes, and asked what it all meant, and would, at that moment, I know, have rather died the night before than see the sun rise on such a day as this.

And so the day wore on, and the sun went down, and with it the hopes of a people who, with prayers, and tears, and blood, had striven to uphold that falling flag.

It was all too true, and our worst fears were fully justified by the result. The suspension of hostilities was but a prelude to surrender, which was, when it came to a show of hands, inevitable.

General Lee's army had been literally pounded to pieces after the battle of "Five Forks," around Petersburg, which made the evacuation of Richmond and the retreat a necessity. When General Longstreet's corps from the north bank joined it, the "army of Northern Virginia," wasted and reduced to skeleton battalions, was still an army of veteran material, powerful yet for attack or defence, all the more dangerous from its desperate condition. And General Grant so recognized and dealt with it, attacking it, as before stated, in detail; letting it wear itself out by straggling and the disorganizing effect of a retreat, breaking down of men and material. The infantry were almost starved.

It was not until the fourth day from Richmond, at the high bridge on the "Appomattox," the battle of Sailor's Creek was fought, in which, with overwhelming masses of cavalry, artillery and infantry, our starved and tired men were ridden down, and General Grant destroyed, in military parlance, the divisions of Kershaw, Ewell, Anderson and Custis Lee.

The fighting next day was of the same desultory character as before, and the day after there was no blow struck until we encountered with the artillery Custar's cavalry, at the depot of Appomattox Court-house, as has been described—all their energies being directed toward establishing their "cordon" around that point.

The terms of the surrender, and all about it, are too well known to go over in detail here—prisoners of war on parole, officers to retain side arms, and all private property to be respected, that was favorable to our cavalry, as in the Confederate service the men all owned their horses, though different in the United States army, the horses belonging to Government.

General Gary, true to the doctrine he had laid down in his discussion with the irate captain, that "South Carolinians did not surrender," turned his horse's head, and, with Captain Doby and one or two others, managed to get that night through the "cordon" drawn around us, and succeeded in reaching Charlotte, North Carolina, which became, for a time, the headquarters of the "Southern Confederacy"—the President and his Cabinet having established themselves there.

Colonel Haskell, who had been separated from us the night before, while gathering up the horses of the brigade, by the charge of cavalry on the turnpike, and had joined and been acting with General Walker and his artillery, came in about two o'clock. All the Confederate cavalry at Appomattox, some two thousand or twenty-five hundred, were under his command as ranking officer.

The brigade crossed the road and bivouacked in the open field near the creek, within a few hundred yards of the town. Our infantry, and what was left of the artillery, was scattered along the road for two or three miles toward Richmond—the enemy swarming in every direction around us, and occupying the town as headquarters.

The articles of capitulation were signed next morning under the famous "apple tree," I suppose; what we saw of it was this: General Lee was seen, dressed in full Confederate uniform, with his sword on, riding his fine grey charger, and accompanied by General Gordon, coming from the village, and riding immediately in front of where we were lying. He had not been particularly noticed as he had gone toward the town, for, though with the regiment, I have no recollection of his doing so. As soon as he was seen it acted like an electric flash upon our men; they sprang to their feet, and, running to the roadside, commenced a wild cheering that roused our troops. As far as we could see they came running down the hill sides, and joining in, along the ground, and through the woods, and up into the sky, there went a tribute that has seldom been paid to mortal man. "Faithful, though all was lost!"

The Federal army officers and men bore themselves toward us as brave men should. I do not recollect, within my personal observation, a single act that could be called discourteous—nor did I hear of one. On the other hand, much kindness and consideration were exhibited when circumstances made it warrantable—such as previous acquaintance, as was common among the officers of the old army, or a return of kindness when parties had been prisoners in our hands, as was the case with a portion of the Seventh regiment when it was the cavalry battalion of the Holcomb Legion, under Colonel Shingler, and the Fifth Pennsylvania cavalry.

Regular rations were issued to men and horses. An apology was offered, on one occasion, by the Federal Quartermaster, for not serving out horse feed, as General F. Lee's division of cavalry, who were, as I mentioned before, outside, up in the James River direction, had cut off a wagon train that held their provender, so we had to send out a forage detail in the neighborhood, with a pass from General Sheridan, to get through the Federal troops that filled the woods for miles around, for their name was legion. We stacked eight thousand stands of arms, all told; artillery, cavalry, infantry stragglers, wagon-rats, and all the rest, from twelve to fifteen thousand men. The United States troops, by their own estimate, were 150,000 men, with a railroad connecting their rear with Washington, New York, Germany, France, Belgium, Africa, "all the world and the rest of man-kind," as General Taylor comprehensively remarked, for their recruiting stations were all over the world, and the crusade against the South, and its peculiar manners and civilization, under the pressure of the "almighty American dollar," was as absolute and varied in its nationality as was that of "Peter the Hermit," under the pressure of religious zeal, upon Jerusalem.

Success had made them good natured. Those we came in contact with were soldiers—fighting men—and, as is always the case, such appreciate their position and are too proud to bear themselves in any other way. They, in the good nature of success, were more willing to give than our men, in the soreness of defeat, to receive.

The effect of such conduct upon our men was of the best kind; the unexpected consideration shown by the officers and men of the United States army towards us; the heartiness with which a Yankee soldier would come up to a Confederate officer and say, "We have been fighting one another for four years; give me a Confederate five dollar bill to remember you by," had nothing in it offensive.

They were proud of their success, and we were not ashamed of our defeat; and not a man of that grand army of one hundred and fifty thousand men but could, and I believe would, testify, that, on purely personal grounds, the few worn-out half-starved men that gathered around General Lee and his falling flag held the prouder position of the two. Had the politicians left things alone, such feelings would have resulted in a very different condition of things.

Those of us who took serious consideration of the state of affairs, felt that with our defeat we had as absolutely lost our country—the one we held under the Constitution—as though we had been conquered and made a colony of by France or Russia. The right of the strongest—the law of the sword—was as absolute at "Appomattox" that day as when Brennus, the Gaul, threw it in the scale at the ransom of Rome.

So far, it was all according to the order of things, and we stood on the bare hills men without a country. General Grant offered us, it was said, rations and transportation—each man to his native State, now a conquered province, or to Halifax, Nova Scotia. Many would not have hesitated to accept the offer for Halifax and rations; but, in distant Southern homes were old men, helpless women and children, whose cry for help it was not hard to hear. So, in good faith, accepting our fate, we took allegiance to this, our new country, which is now called the "United States," as we would have done to France or Russia.

With all that was around us—the destruction of the "Army of Northern Virginia," and certain defeat of the Confederacy as the result—no one dreamed of what has followed. The fanaticism that has influenced the policy of the Government, to treat subject States, whose citizens had been permitted to take an oath of allegiance, accepted them as such, and promised to give them the benefit of laws protecting person, property and religion, as the dominant party in the United States has done— exceeds belief.

To place the government of the States absolutely in the hands of its former slaves, and call their "acts" "laws;" to denounce the slightest effort to assert the white vote, even under the laws, treason; and, finally, force the unwilling United States soldier to use his bayonet to sustain the grossest outrages of law and decency against men of his own color and race! This has gone on until, lost in wonder as to what is to come next, the southern white man watches events, as a tide that is gradually rising and spreading, and from which he sees no avenue of escape, and must, unless an intervention almost miraculous takes place, soon sweep him away.

Lee in Richmond, shortly after Appomattox

The Fourth Massachusetts Cavalry in the Closing Scenes of the War for the Maintenance of the Union, from Richmond to Appomattox

Told in four parts:
The Battle at High Bridge
The First United States Flag Raised In Richmond After the War
The Fourth Massachusetts Cavalry: In the Closing Scenes of the War for the Maintenance of the Union, From Richmond to Appomattox
Death of the War Horse

Col. Arnold A. Rand
4th Massachusetts Volunteer Cavalry

The Battle at High Bridge
by
Major Edward T. Bouvé, U. S. V.

The life of the American Cavalry is almost coeval with that of the American people. Laws were passed for the formation of a mounted force in 1648, when the colony of Massachusetts Bay had not yet attained its majority. Twenty-seven years later, in 1675, when the war with Metacomet (King Philip) broke out there were five troops of cavalry, which in point of equipment, discipline and appearance, had received the commendation of European officers who had seen them.

Captain Prentice's troop formed a part of Major-General Winslow's army, which fought at Narrangansett Fort. It participated in the terrible march and the awful battle which ensued. Of that battle, the latest and most exhaustive of its historians says:

"This must be classed as one of the most glorious victories ever achieved in our history, and considering conditions, as displaying heroism both in stubborn patience and dashing intrepidity never excelled in American warfare."

So much for the first great battle in which Massachusetts cavalry took an honorable part. I may be pardoned for referring to it in this paper, on account of the singular coincidence, that in one of the last, and unquestionably one of the most brilliant actions ever fought in America—the Battle at High Bridge—Massachusetts horsemen accomplished a very difficult thing: they succeeded in adding a yet deeper lustre to the laurels which have ever adorned the standards of the American Cavalry.

The story of the fight near High Bridge, Virginia, is but an account of an obscure skirmish, if the numbers engaged and its duration be solely considered; judged, however, by the fierce intensity of the struggle, and the carnage, together with the results, which alone, yet amply, justified the apparent madness of the attack, it is seen to be one of the most notable of the achievements of those heroic days; for it led to the culmination of the campaign and end of the war, at Appomattox. It was called by Mr. Hay and Mr. Nicolay, in their history of Abraham Lincoln, the most gallant and pathetic battle of the war.

The Fourth Regiment of Massachusetts Cavalry had been subjected to a training and discipline which caused it to develop rapidly into one of the finest cavalry regiments in the army. The officers were nearly all veteran soldiers, educated in the hard school of war. A large proportion of the men in the ranks had seen service, and the rank and file, as a whole, proved to be such as any officer might be proud to lead.

The quality of the regiment is easily accounted for, when it is considered that its first colonel left the lasting impress of himself upon it; that colonel was Arnold A. Rand.

From the very beginning of its service in the field, the regiment had the hard fortune to be cut up into detachments and details for special duty. This was probably due to the good opinion entertained of it by the general; but it was very trying and disappointing to the colonel, and to all who had hoped to be serving, as earlier orders—too soon countermanded—directed, with Sheridan.

At the opening of the last campaign, the first and third battalions were in Virginia. Three squadrons, with the field and staff, were attached to the headquarters of General Ord, commanding the Army of the James; two were at the headquarters of the Twenty-fourth, and two at those of the Twenty-fifth Army corps. One was at Fort Magruder, where it had been for many months, doing outpost and picket duty and engaged in scouting and raiding. The second battalion was in active service in South Carolina and Florida.

Before the spring campaign opened, the command of the regiment had passed to Francis Washburn of Lancaster, a member of a family distinguished for its public services. This young gentleman was a patrician in the best sense of the word. With the most brilliant prospects in life, he, like his brother, left all to serve the Republic, and both drew "the gret prize o' death in battle."

In physical proportions, in personal beauty, in superb daring, in high-minded devotion to every duty, he was the ideal of a cavalry leader, and a worthy successor to the first regimental commander.

One of the worst features of the internal economy of our armies during the civil war, was the detailing of officers and men individually from fighting regiments; the officers to serve on staff, the men for orderlies, wagoners, hospital service and other special duties which reduced the fighting strength to a minimum compared with what it should have been. Probably the same custom would rule now.

Owing to this pernicious, although at the time unavoidable system, as well as to the ordinary casualties of the service, the three squadrons of the Fourth Cavalry under the immediate command of Colonel Washburn at the beginning of active service, had been reduced to one hundred and fifty men.

Orders were issued on the 27th of March to break camp, preparatory to the resumption of movements against the lines of communication between the besieged cities and their sources of supply.

Richmond and Petersburg were evacuated on the third of April, General Lee moving swiftly toward Amelia. The Federal armies marched at once in hot pursuit, the Army of the James taking the general direction of the Lynchburg railroad, reaching Burkesville on the evening of April 5th. That same evening, Lee left Amelia Court house, pushing rapidly in the direction of High Bridge, a long trestle over the Appomattox near Farmville. Could he reach this bridge, cross and destroy it, he might hope to succeed in gaining the mountains beyond Lynchburg.

The Army of the James instantly changed direction in pursuit. Lee's objective point became evident, and General Ord determined to destroy the bridge, if it were possible to accomplish this, before Lee could reach it. To this end, he detached Colonel Washburn, with the three squadrons of his own cavalry, now reduced by further details to thirteen officers and sixty-seven troopers, together with two small regiments of infantry, and directed him to push on rapidly and burn the bridge.

Information had been received through scouts that the structure was not defended by any fortifications whatever. Reports also came in that the Confederates were badly demoralized. In consequence of these stories, which would appear to have been accepted as fully reliable at headquarters, Washburn was ordered to attack any force which he might meet, as it would certainly fall away before him.

It was a perilous order to give Washburn, for his valor was ever the better part of his discretion.

Some of our generals seem to have been strangely misled as to the spirit of the Confederates remaining in arms. Never had they fought more fiercely than in those last days of the struggle. Their skeleton battalions threw themselves upon our heavy lines at Sailor's Creek as desperately as they charged under Pickett and Edward Johnson at Gettysburg, and their artillery was never more superbly served than when they were attacked in flank by Gregg's brigade on the seventh of April, when that general was made prisoner and his brigade driven in complete discomfiture by the famous Washington Artillery of New Orleans.

On the morning of the sixth, before dawn, Washburn's little detachment took up its route, the infantry, especially, being in poor condition for the severe and peculiarly dangerous service to which they were called, for they were exhausted by the forced marches which had been indispensable during the preceding three days. The distance was sixteen miles to Farmville. After having been two hours or so upon the road, Washburn satisfied himself that the rebel army, moving diagonally toward the Appomattox, had closed in upon his rear, cutting him off from the Army of the James. There were also unmistakable indications that Confederate columns were moving in front of his command, as well as on its flank. The detachment was thus marching practically among divisions of the enemy, who were evidently ignorant of its proximity.

Meanwhile, General Ord had learned of the movements of the Confederates, and at once despatched Brevet Brigadier General Theodore Read, adjutant general of the Army of the James, to overtake

Washburn and cause him to fall back to the main army. Read, with one orderly, contrived to elude the various bodies of the enemy and finally joined Washburn, just before his command reached the vicinity of the bridge.

Upon reconnoitering the country about the bridge, it was found that the information as to its not being fortified was entirely false. A strong redoubt mounting four guns protected it, and the ground around it was open, with morasses in front rendering it almost impossible of access. Washburn considered, however, that a sudden attack on its rear side by cavalry, might be successful.

In pursuance of this plan, he left Read with the infantry in a narrow belt of woodland near the Burkesville road, and moved away to make a detour in order to come upon the rear of the fortification.

The column soon reached a small stream spanned by a bridge, the planks of which had been torn up. Lieutenant Davis with the advanced guard, dashed across the stream and laid the planks under sharp fire from a force of dismounted cavalry which occupied low earthworks on the further side. Washburn soon came up with the main body, and throwing out a line of skirmishers, attacked so vigorously that after a fight of half an hour's duration, the enemy retreated toward Farmville. Here they were reinforced, and Washburn soon found their numbers so great and their artillery fire so heavy, that they could not be driven. Moreover there was incessant musketry firing from the place where he had left the infantry, indicating an attack upon them, and he thought best to withdraw and go to their support.

A sharp ride of a few moments brought the cavalry to the scene of action. Had the Burkesville road been followed for a short distance farther the column would have rounded a bend in the road, and come upon a strong body of Confederate cavalry which was moving in the direction of the firing; but at a point in rear of where the fighting was going on, Washburn left the road and led his men through the woods and along the bed of a ravine, then up a hill, where he halted to learn the state of affairs.

Col. Francis Washburn

The little line of infantry, outflanked and outnumbered, was falling back fighting, pushed by a brigade of dismounted cavalry, while regiments of horse were galloping up on the flanks and forming for a charge. The infantry were clearly exhausted and their ammunition was used up, but Washburn, after a short consultation with Read, sent his adjutant to rally them, and determined by a furious attack upon the dismounted troops of the enemy, to throw them back on their cavalry and thus, supported by the infantry, to wrest victory from the enemy. He then led the column along the crest of the slope, and forming line, turned to his men and explained his purpose, well knowing what he could expect from the splendid fellows.

Then Washburn ordered "Forward!" The line trotted down the slope. In a moment came his clear call "Gallop, march! Charge!" And to the music from the brazen throats of their own trumpets chiming with their fierce battle shout, those seventy-eight Massachusetts horsemen hurled themselves upon the heavy masses of the foe.

For a few moments the air was bright with the flashing of sabres, and shattered by the explosion of carbine and pistol, while screams of rage mingled with the cries of the wounded and all the hideous sounds of a savage hand-to-hand fight. As all this died away, it was seen that the immediate body of troops which the Fourth Cavalry had struck was practically annihilated. Their dead and wounded were scattered thickly over the field, while the crowd of prisoners taken was embarrassing to the captors. Driving these before them back toward the hill, to which they must retire to reform for attack upon the enemy's horse (for Washburn's mere handful of men forbade his leaving any to form the reserve without which cavalry almost never can charge without great risk) they were astounded at the sight which presented itself on the Burkesville road. As far as the eye could reach, it was filled with Confederate cavalry, and lines of battle were forming as rapidly as possible and advancing swiftly to the aid of their defeated van.

All hope of victory or of escape from such a field was now utterly gone, but the colonel and his men were mad with the fury of battle, and wild with exultation over the bloody triumph already achieved. But one thought possessed them. The little battalion swept down the slope once more, pressing close behind their knightly leader and their blue standard.

They crashed through three lines of their advancing enemies, tearing their formation asunder as the tornado cuts its way through the forest. But now, order and coherence were lost, and the troopers mingled with the Confederates in a bitter hand-to-hand struggle. A few scattered fighters were rallied from out this fearful melée by the gallant Captain Hodges, than whom a more chivalrous soldier never drew sabre. He led them in a last furious charge, in which he fell, as he would have wished, "amid the battle's wildest tide."

By this time, all was lost. Eight of the officers lay dead or wounded upon the field. Three were prisoners, their horses having been killed under them. The surgeon and chaplain, being non-combatants, were captured while in attendance upon the wounded.

The battle at High Bridge was finished, for General Read had been mortally wounded at the first fire after the infantry had rallied in support of the cavalry attack, and the two small regiments were overwhelmed and compelled to surrender as soon as the cavalry had ceased to be a factor.

Colonel Washburn had been shot in the mouth and sabred as he fell from his horse. He was found on the field with the other dead and wounded the next day, when the advance of the Army of the James came up. He was taken to the hospital at Point of Rocks but insisted upon being sent to his home in Massachusetts, where he died in the arms of his mother. Before his death, he was, at Grant's request, brevetted as Brigadier General.

Of the other officers, Lieutenant Colonel Jenkins was severely wounded, as were Captain Caldwell and Lieutenants Belcher and Thompson. Captains Hodges and Goddard were killed, and Lieutenant Davis shot after having been made a prisoner, for resenting an insult offered him by a rebel officer. The adjutant, Lieutenant Lathrop, after his horse had been killed under him, was taken into the woods to be shot, because his captor asserted that he had slain his brother in the fight. Fortunately a Confederate staff-officer observed the proceeding, and rescued him from his would-be murderer.

Happily, the casualties among the enlisted men were much less in proportion than among the officers. They had to a man fought with the most desperate valor, keeping up the struggle after all the officers were down, until absolutely ingulfed in the masses of the enemy.

In telling of the practical annihilation of a body of troops, the statement that their standard was saved from capture seems almost incredible; yet such was the case in this instance. The color sergeant, a gallant soldier from Hingham by the name of Thomas Hickey, had carried the standard through the hottest of the battle. At the last moment, seeing that it was impossible to save it from capture except by destroying it, he managed to elude the enemies who were closing in upon him, and putting spurs to his horse, flew toward a hut which he had observed in the woods, and threw himself from his charger just as he reached it, with his foes close upon him. Rushing it, he thrust his precious battle flag into a fire which was blazing on the hearth. The painted silk flashed up in flame, and by the time that his pursuers broke in, it was ashes!

His life was spared in consideration of his devoted bravery, and he subsequently received a commission from the Governor of the Commonwealth, in recognition of his heroic deed.

The losses of the Confederates in this action were at least a half greater in number than Washburn's whole force. By their own report, there were a hundred killed and wounded, among them a general, one colonel, three majors and a number of officers of lower grade.

The Battle at High Bridge was at first thought to have been a useless sacrifice. It was a sacrifice indeed, but it unquestionably hastened the termination of the war, by days, and perhaps weeks.

After the surrender, Lee's Inspector General said to Ord,

"To the sharpness of that fight, the cutting off of Lee's army at Appomattox was probably owing. So fierce were the charges of Colonel Washburn and his men, and so determined their fighting, that General Lee received the impression that they must be supported by a large part of the army, and that his retreat was cut off."

Lee consequently halted and began to intrench; and this delay gave time for Ord to come up, and enabled Sheridan to intercept the enemy at

Sailor's Creek.

The Confederate General Rosser said to a member of the regiment whom he met after the war:

"You belonged to the Fourth Massachusetts Cavalry? Give me your hand! I have been many a day in hot fights. I never saw anything approaching that at High Bridge. While your colonel kept his saddle, everything went down before him!"

The Confederate troops at High Bridge were Rosser's and a part of Fitz Hugh Lee's divisions.

"Was your colonel drunk or crazy this morning, that he attacked with less than one hundred men the best fighting division of the Confederate cavalry?" asked a rebel officer of a wounded captain of the Fourth; "We have seen hard fighting, but we never heard of anything like this before!"

The Confederate officers had at first utterly refused to credit the stories of their prisoners, insisting that the small force would never have fought so fiercely unless it had been the advance of a strong column.

Grant says in his memoirs.

"The Confederates took this to be only the advance of a larger column which had headed them off, and so stopped to intrench; so that this gallant band had checked the progress of a strong detachment of the Confederate army. This stoppage of Lee's column no doubt saved to us the trains following."

Major Atherton H. Stevens
4th Mass. Volunteer Cavalry

The First United States Flag Raised In Richmond After the War

By
Mrs. Lasalle Corbell Pickett,
Wife of Major-General George E. Pickett, C. S. A.

The first knell of the evacuation of Richmond sounded on Sunday morning while we were on our knees in St. Paul's Church, invoking God's protecting care for our absent loved ones, and blessings on our cause.

The intense excitement, the tolling of the bells, the hasty parting, the knowledge that all communication would be cut off between us and our loved ones, and the dread, undefined fear in our helplessness and desertion, make a nightmare memory.

General Ewell had orders for the destruction of the public buildings, which orders our Secretary of War, Gen. J. C. Breckenridge strove earnestly but without avail to have countermanded. The order, alas! was obeyed beyond the "letter of the law."

The terrible conflagration was kindled by the Confederate authorities, who applied the torch to the Shockoe warehouse, it, too, being classed among the public buildings because of the tobacco belonging to France and England stored in it. A fresh breeze was blowing from the south; the fire swept on in its haste and fury over a great area in an almost incredibly short time, and by noon the flames had transformed into a desert waste all the city bounded by Seventh and Fifteenth Streets, and Main Street and the river. One thousand houses were destroyed. The streets were filled with furniture and every description of wares, dashed down to be trampled in the mud or buried where they lay.

At night a saturnalia began. About dark, the Government commissary began the destruction of its stores. Soldiers and citizens gathered in front, catching the liquor in basins and pitchers; some with their hats and some with their boots. It took but a short time for this to make a manifestation as dread as the flames. The crowd became a howling mob, so frenzied that the officers of the law had to flee for their lives, reviving memories of 1781, when the British under Arnold rode down Richmond Hill, and, invading the city, broke open the stores and emptied the provisions and liquors into the gutters, making even the uninitiated cows and hogs drunk for days.

All through the night, crowds of men, women, and children traversed the streets, loading themselves with supplies and plunder. At midnight, soldiers drunk with vile liquor, followed by a reckless crowd as drunk as themselves, dashed in the plate-glass windows of the stores, and made a wreck of everything.

About nine o'clock on Monday morning, terrific shell explosions, rapid and continuous, added to the terror of the scene, and gave the impression that the city was being shelled by the retreating Confederate army from the south side. But the explosions were soon found to proceed from the Government arsenal and laboratory, then in flames. Later in the morning, a merciful Providence caused a lull in the breeze. The terrific explosion of the laboratory and of the arsenal caused every window in our home to break. The old plate-glass mirrors, built in the walls, were cracked and shattered.

Fort Darling was blown up, and later on the rams. It was eight o'clock when the Federal troops entered the city. It required the greatest effort to tame down the riotous, crazed mob, and induce them to take part in the struggle to save their own. The firemen, afraid of the soldiers who had obeyed the orders to light the torch, would not listen to any appeals or entreaties, and so the flames were under full headway, fanned by a southern breeze, when the Union soldiers came to the rescue.

The flouring mills caught fire from the tobacco houses, communicating it to Cary and Main streets. Every bank was destroyed. The War Department was a mass of ruins; the Enquirer and Dispatch offices were in ashes; and the county court-house, the American Hotel, and most of the finest stores of the city were ruined.

Libby Prison and the Presbyterian church escaped. Such a reign of terror and pillage, fire and flame, fear and despair! The yelling and howling and swearing and weeping and wailing beggar description. Families houseless and homeless under the open sky!

I shall never forget General Weitzel's command, composed exclusively of colored troops, as I saw them through the dense black columns of smoke. General Weitzel had for some time been stationed on the north side of the James River, but a few miles from Richmond, and he had only to march in and take possession. He despatched Major A. H. Stevens of the Fourth Massachusetts cavalry, and Major E. E. Graves of his staff, with about a hundred mounted men, to reconnoitre the roads and works leading to Richmond. They had gone but a little distance into the Confederate lines, when they saw a shabby, old-fashioned carriage, drawn by a pair of lean, lank horses, the occupants waving a white flag. They met this flag-of-truce party at the line of fortifications, just beyond the junction of the Osborne turnpike and New Market road. The carriage contained the mayor of Richmond—Colonel Mayo—Judge Meredith of the Supreme Court, and Judge Lyons. The fourth worthy I cannot recall. Judge Lyons, our former minister to England, and one of the representative men of Virginia, made the introductions in his own characteristic way, and then Colonel Mayo, who was in command of the flag-of-truce party, handed to Major Stevens a small slip of wall paper, on which was written the following: "It is proper to formally surrender to the Federal authorities the city of Richmond, hitherto capital of the Confederate States of America, and the defenses protecting it up to this time." That was all. The document was approved of, and Major Stevens most courteously accepted the terms for his commanding general, to whom it was at once transmitted, and moved his column upon the evacuated city, taking possession and saving it from ashes.

His first order was to sound the alarm bells and to take command at once of the fire department, which consisted of fourteen substitute men, those who were exempt from service because of disease, two steam fire engines, four worthless hand engines, and a large amount of hose, destroyed by the retreating half-crazed Confederates. His next order was to raise the stars and stripes over the Capitol. Quick as thought, two soldiers, one from Company E and one from Company H of the Fourth Massachusetts cavalry, crept to the summit and planted the flag of the nation. Two bright, tasteful guidons were hoisted by the halyards in place of the red cross. The living colors of the Union were greeted, while our "Warriors' banner took its flight to meet the warrior's soul."

That flag, whose design has been accredited alike to both George Washington and John Adams, was raised over Virginia by Massachusetts, in place of the one whose kinship and likeness had not, even after renewed effort, been entirely destroyed. For by the adoption of the stars and bars (three horizontal bars of equal width—the middle one white, the others red—with a blue union of nine stars in a circle) by the Confederate Congress in March, 1861, the Confederate flag was made so akin and so similar to that of the nation, as to cause confusion; so in 1863 the stars and bars was supplanted by a flag with a white field, having the battle flag (a red field charged with a blue saltier, on which were thirteen stars) for a union. This, having been mistaken for a flag of truce, was altered by covering the outer half of the field beyond the union with a vertical red bar. This was the last flag of the Confederacy.

Richmond will testify that the soldiers of Massachusetts were worthy of the honor of raising the first United States flag over her Capitol—the Capitol of the Confederacy—and also to the unvarying courtesy of Major Stevens, and the fidelity with which he kept his trust.

Capt. A. F. Ray

The Fourth Massachusetts Cavalry In the Closing Scenes of the War for the Maintenance of the Union, From Richmond to Appomattox.

By

WM. B. ARNOLD,

Formerly Company H 4th Massachusetts Cavalry.

During the winter and spring of 1864 and 1865 squadrons E and H of the 4th Massachusetts cavalry were encamped near the headquarters of General Weitzel commanding the Twenty-fifth Army Corps, then a part of the Army of the James. Our command was detached from our regiment and doing duty as orderlies and couriers at Division and Brigade headquarters and Artillery Brigade headquarters, as well as performing Provost duty at corps headquarters.

Our command numbered about eighty men in charge of Captain A. F. Ray of Company H, 4th Massachusetts cavalry. He was an officer of unusual ability. The Army of the James held possession north of the James, their lines extending from Deep Bottom, a few miles below Dutch Gap to Fort Harrison and around to the New Market road.

Our position was made very strong and withstood the attack of the Confederates several times after it was taken from them in Sept. 1864. Their defenses in our front were equally strong. In addition they had several iron clads in the James River to assist in the defense of Richmond. Our gunboats were down the river, none of them, up to this time, having ventured above the Dutch Gap canal.

The afternoon and evening of April second, 1865 indicated that something unusual was likely to occur. The Artillery firing in the direction of Petersburg in the evening, and during the night of the second was heavy and continuous, and in the night the sky was lighted up toward Richmond which proved to be the Ram Virginia on fire. When the fire reached the magazine there was a tremendous explosion. Soon after this it was reported that the Confederates were evacuating the works in our front. An order came from General Weitzel for a detail of fifty cavalry which was immediately mounted, and reported at corps headquarters.

We were commanded by Captain A. F. Ray of H squadron, accompanied by officers from Twenty-fifth army corps headquarters, and the entire command in charge of Major Atherton H. Stevens of the 4th Massachusetts cavalry and Provost Marshall of the 25th Army Corps.

We proceeded at once through our fortified line and approaching the Confederate line found that the troops were gone. Working our way several miles toward Richmond, we could see through the fog a body of Confederate infantry. Major Stevens immediately ordered a charge, and Captain Ray quickly responded with his men. At our near approach they surrendered. We continued "on to Richmond," and were soon inside the inner works that were impregnable when manned by a sufficient number for defence. With deep ditches and fallen trees to entangle attacking parties, the Artillery and Infantry commanded the approach in every direction without exposing themselves.

The elaborate preparations for defense kept our armies at bay for months around Petersburg, and Richmond was prepared for standing off superior numbers by the best earthworks that our West Point engineers who were in the Confederate army could devise. As we entered these works we saw a man approaching with a flag of truce.

In the distance were mounted men and carriages. We halted and Major Stevens and his officers went forward and conferred with the party, who proved to be the Mayor of Richmond accompanied by Judge Medereth and other prominent people of Richmond. The city was formally surrendered to Major Stevens and we then went forward at a rapid pace, and coming round a turn in the roadway at the Rockets, came in full view of Richmond.

We halted for a moment to contemplate the scene. A portion of the city toward the James river was on fire. The black smoke was rolling up in great volumes. Major Stevens said "everyone of us should feel as proud as if we were promoted to be Brigadier Generals." We gave three cheers and went on, and were soon in the streets of Richmond passing Libby Prison; and we clattered up the paved street on the gallop to the Capitol, and were soon in the space in front of the Capitol building.

Major Stevens, with some of the officers, rushed into the building, and soon the guidons of Company E and H were fluttering from the top of the building. We were formed around the equestrian statue of Washington, and we gave three times three, and a Tiger, that indicated to spectators that we were there. Richmond was ours, after four long years of tremendous struggle and sacrifice. I, for one, thought of the splendid services of thousands of the best troops ever rallied to maintain a just cause. That our detail was privileged to land first in Richmond with the flags of Massachusetts, was certainly appreciated by us.

But our work was not over. A large area of the city toward the river was on fire. To add to the fury of the flames the Arsenals were blowing up and the shells were continually exploding. Corporal Macy and myself went with Captain Ray to ascertain if the bridges connecting Richmond with Manchester were destroyed by the evacuating Confederates.

We went up Main street to Eighth street and then across to Cary street, and turned to the South, and went by burning buildings until we obtained a view of the bridges. The two bridges were on fire, and burning rapidly from the Manchester side. Everything in front of us was on fire; buildings blowing up and flames roaring in every direction.

We started back and observed on our left a fire in a building which was stored with ammunition. We galloped past the building and turned the corner toward Main street nearby when the building exploded. As we emerged from the smoke and cinders, Captain Ray remarked that we had only five seconds to spare and a close shave, even where we were when the building went up. We returned to the Capitol and reported to Major Stevens. I was sent with a detail to the Davis Mansion with instructions to leave a guard on the house. I found everything unmolested.

The desk used by the Confederate President was in disorder and everything indicated a hasty departure. I returned to my company, and we were kept busy in restoring order. Soon our troops began to pour into the city and order reigned. Energetic measures to stop the destruction of the city were promptly taken. The blue lines looked good to me, and the people soon realized that instead of destroyers they were saviors, for they saved the city not already burned by the folly of the retreating Confederates.

When we arrived in Richmond there was disorder, frenzy and chaos on every hand. Major Stevens restored order and confidence in a remarkably short time under conditions that were most trying. The troops as they arrived, were distributed where they could work effectively. Streets and residences were immediately guarded. The soldiers did not leave their commands to enrich themselves, and perfect order was restored before nightfall. Our little band of cavalry was everywhere, and making good for lack of numbers by energetic performance until the arrival of the infantry. And after they came we were in the saddle till late at night.

We encamped for the night in the yard of the Female Institute building, and we were a tired but happy band. The next day, April 4th, was quiet. The infernal condition of fire, smoke and explosion and continuous bursting of shells was changed to a scene of waste and ruin wrought in the fire district, which covered about one third of the city. The day was made eventful by the appearance of President Lincoln in the city. He came up from City Point and walked up the street alone with his boy. General Devens immediately received him. Mr. Lincoln met with a splendid ovation from the troops and the colored people as he rode about the city. He rode in a carriage accompanied by General Devens and other officers, escorted by a detail of cavalry from E and H squadrons of the 4th Massachusetts cavalry, commanded by Captain A. F. Ray.

On the morning of April 5th, the detachment that composed the detail that first entered Richmond on the morning of April 3, 1865, started to join its regiment, commanded by Colonel Washburn. They were with General Ord commanding the army of the James in pursuit of General Lee's retreating forces. We proceeded by way of Petersburg through Dinwiddie County and Amelia Courthouse to Burkeville Junction, arriving there April 7th. There we found that Colonel Washburn's command was engaged at High Bridge the day before, meeting with heavy loss, but emerging from the conflict with much honor and a splendid record of achievement.

The engagement is well described by our comrade, Captain Bouve of the 4th Massachusetts cavalry and will interest surviving comrades of the regiment, and all who love the defenders of their country. Colonel Washburn and many others of our regiment were in the field hospital at Burkeville Junction and Captain Ray and Lieutenant Miller visited them, and returning to our camp, gave us a graphic description of the charges of our comrades the day before. Colonel Washburn survived his injuries only a few days. He told Captain Ray that "if I had the whole of the 4th regiment with me I would have annihilated Fitz Hugh Lee and Rosser." This was the marvelous courage and spirit of the man, "a gentleman and a soldier."

We immediately started on to report to the headquarters of the army of the Potomac. All the way from Petersburg there was evidence of conflict. At Amelia Courthouse we found the remnants of Ewell's corps of the Confederate army. Artillery, wagons and ammunition piled up in disorder; from people along the way reports of fighting. The Confederate troops hurriedly passed down the highway, to be immediately followed by the blue lines of federal troops. On the morning of the ninth of April we began to catch up with the army of the Potomac.

Through the lines of the sixth and ninth corps we rode, until early in the afternoon came the report that Lee had surrendered. You ought to have seen the faces of the soldiers of the army of the Potomac then. They looked like heroes to me. When we reached the Confederate lines we kept on through their camps and landed at General Meade's headquarters at Appomattox C. H., where we were immediately put on duty to assist in the work of paroling and disbanding the Confederate army.

A detail from my squadron went to Lynchburg one afternoon with General Gibbons returning in the night. When the arrangements of paroling the Confederate army were complete and General Lee was at liberty to depart from his army, an order came from army headquarters for a detail of cavalry to escort General Lee from his lines. The escort was made up from the 4th Massachusetts cavalry and I was privileged to be one of them. Sixteen men composed the platoon and Lieutenant Lovell of our regiment was in command. I was right guide of the detail, and I thought at the time that we were pretty good representatives of the Union cavalry.

We had H guidon with us which was one of the flags that was the first in Richmond. We went to General Lee's headquarters and Lieutenant Lovell reported to General Lee.

He was courteously received and asked to wait until General Lee and his staff had breakfast and completed arrangements for their departure. We dismounted a short distance away. General Lee seated himself at a table made from a hard tack box and ate his last breakfast (consisting of hard tack, fried pork and coffee without milk), with the army of Northern Virginia. He was dressed in a neat, gray uniform and was a splendid looking soldier. Commanding officers of corps and divisions of the Confederate army and other officers then came to take leave of him. He was a short distance from me and his conversation was evidently words of encouragement and advice. Almost every one of the officers went away in tears. Then we mounted, and General Lee's party started through the lines of the remnant of the Army of Northern Virginia for his home in Richmond.

Then commenced an ovation that seemed to me a wonderful manifestation of confidence and affection for this great military chieftain. From the time we left his camp till we passed the last of his regiments the men seemed to come from everywhere and the "Rebel Yell" was continuous. The little guidon of our squadron fluttered in the breeze and seemed silently to voice the sentiment of Webster, "Liberty and Union now and forever, one and inseparable."

The war was truly over and General Lee was departing for his home to devote the remainder of his life in peaceful pursuits. We continued with him a short distance in Buckingham County where the party halted. General Lee rode up to Lieutenant Lovell and thanked him for the escort, and saluted as he went his way, while we returned to Appomattox. At night the army of Northern Virginia was gone. The Union army was preparing to take up the line of march for their homes. The years of achievement and sacrifice have been commented on by eloquent orators. I have endeavored to pen a simple narrative to mention events as they appeared to me.

When the army started from Appomattox they were rejoiced to contemplate changed conditions. At night camp fires were burning. The dangerous duty of picket and scouting and fighting was a thing of the past. Everybody felt elated and happy.

The news of President Lincoln's assassination came, and quiet and sadness reigned. It seemed a great pity that this should come to put a nation in mourning, at a time when rejoicing for the Nation redeemed, was universal. Our detachment returned to Richmond and we remained with our regiment, doing duty in restoring order in and around Petersburg and Richmond until late in the fall of 1865 when we were mustered out, the last Massachusetts Volunteer Regiment to return home.

Death of the War Horse

The Death of the Old War Horse which Col Tilden of the Sixteenth Maine rode during the war, prompted the Rev. Nathaniel Butler to write the following lines.

The sentiment expressed naturally appeals to anyone and especially to a soldier who rode a horse during the war to maintain the Union.

Farewell, my horse! thy work is done,
Thy splendid form lies low,
Thy limbs of steel have lost their strength,
Thy flashing eye its glow.

No more thy quivering nostrils sniff
The battle from afar,
No more beneath thy flying feet
The plains with thunder jar.

For thou wert born a hero soul,
In days when heroes fought,
When men, borne by thy glorious strength,
Immortal laurels sought.

Seated upon thy nerve-strung form,
Another life was mine,
And well I knew the same high thrill
Ran through my soul and thine.

A throne thou wert to sit upon,
And true as steel within,
Whene'er I felt thy brave heart beat,
My own has braver been.

And when the bugle's call to Charge
Over the column ran,
Thy arching crest, "with thunder clothed,"
Loved best to lead the van.

Upon the march, with tireless feet,
Through mountain, gorge and plain,
When others strayed thy place was kept,
Through all the long campaign.

But now, thy last, long halt is made:
Thy last campaign is o'er;
The bugle call, the battle shout
Shall thrill thee never more.

Where art thou gone—old friend and true?
What place hast thou to fill?
For it may be thy spirit form
Somewhere is marching still.

Here there are those whom we call men,
Whose souls full well I know
Another life may not deserve
One-half so well as thou.

And natures such as thine has been
Another life may claim,
And God may have a place for them
Within his wide domain.

His armies tread their glorious march
Over the eternal plain,
Their leader rides a snow white steed,
Who follow in his train?

We may not ever meet again;
But, wheresoe'er I go,
A cherished place within my heart

Thou'lt have, old friend, I know.

God made us both, and we have marched
Firm friends whilst thou wert here;
I only know I shall not blush
To meet thee anywhere.

Selections from the 1866 collection

War Poetry of the South

Edited By
William Gilmore Simms, LL. D.

The Battle of Richmond.
By
George Herbert Sass, Charleston, S.C.

*"For they gat not the land in possession by their own sword; neither
was it their own arm that helped them; but Thy right hand, and Thine
arm, and the light of Thy countenance, because Thou hadst a favor unto
them."*—Psalm, xliv. 3, 4.

I.
Now blessed be the Lord of Hosts through all our Southern land,
And blessed be His holy name, in whose great might we stand;
For He who loves the voice of prayer hath heard His people's cry,
And with His own almighty arm hath won the victory!
Oh, tell it out through hearth and home, from blue Potomac's wave
To those far waters of the West which hide De Soto's grave.

II.
Now let there be through all the land one grand triumphant cry,
Wherever beats a Southern heart, or glows a Southern sky;
For He who ruleth every fight hath been with us to-day,
And the great God of battles hath led the glorious fray;
Oh, then unto His holy name ring out the joyful song,
The race hath not been to the swift, the battle to the strong.

III.
From royal Hudson's cliff-crowned banks, from proud Ohio's flood,
From that dark rock in Plymouth's bay where erst the pilgrims stood,
From East and North, from far and near, went forth the gathering cry,
And the countless hordes came swarming on with fierce and lustful eye.
In the great name of Liberty each thirsty sword is drawn;
In the great name of Liberty each tyrant presseth on.

IV.

Alas, alas! her sacred name is all dishonored now,
And blood-stained hands are tearing off each laurel from her brow;
But ever yet rings out the cry, in loud and mocking tone,
Still in her holy shrine they strive to rear a despot's throne;
And pressing on with eager tread, they sweep across the land,
To burn and havoc and destroy—a fierce and ruthless band.

V.

I looked on fair Potomac's shore, and at my feet the while
The sparkling waves leaped gayly up to meet glad summer's smile;
And pennons gay were floating there, and banners fair to see,
A mighty host arrayed, I ween, in war's proud panoply;
And as I gazed a cry arose, a low, deep-swelling hum,
And loud and stern along the line broke in the sullen drum.

VI.

Onward, o'er fair Virginia's fields, through ranks of nodding grain,
With shout and song they sweep along, a gay and gallant train.
Oh, ne'er, I ween, had those broad plains beheld a fairer sight,
And clear and glad those skies of June shed forth their glorious light.
Onwards, yea, ever onwards, that mighty host hath passed,
And "On to Richmond!" is the cry which echoes on the blast.

VII.

I looked again, the rising sun shines down upon the moors,
And 'neath his beams rise ramparts high and frowning embrasures,
And on each proud abattis yawn, with menace stern and dread,
Grim-visaged messengers of death: the watchful sentry's tread
In measured cadence slowly falls; all Nature seems at ease,
And over all the Stars and Stripes are floating in the breeze.

VIII.

But far away another line is stretching dark and long,
Another flag is floating free where armed legions throng;
Another war-cry's on the air, as wakes the martial drum,
And onward still, in serried ranks, the Southern soldiers come,
And up to that abattis high the charging' columns tread,
And bold and free the Stars and Bars are waving at their head.

IX.

They are on it! they are o'er it! who can stay that living flood?
Lo, ever swelling, rolleth on the weltering tide of blood.
Yet another and another is full boldly stormed and won,
And forward to the spoiler's camp the column presseth on.
Hurrah! hurrah! the field is won! we'e met them man to man,
And ever still the Stars and Bars are riding in the van.

X.

They are flying! they are flying! and close upon their track
Comes our glorious "Stonewall" Jackson, with ten thousand at his back;
And Longstreet, too, and gallant Hill, and Rhodes, and brave Huger,[1]
And he whose name is worth a host, our bold, devoted Lee;
And back to where the lordly James his scornful billow rolls,
The recreant foe is fleeing fast—those men of dastard souls.

XI.

They are flying! they are flying! horse and foot, and bold dragoon,
In one refluent mass are mingled, 'neath the slowly waning moon;
And louder still the cry is heard, as borne upon the blast,
The shouts of the pursuing host are rising full and fast:
"On, on unto the river, 'tis our only chance for life!
We needs must reach the gunboats, or we perish in the strife!"

XII.

'Tis done! the gory field is ours; we've conquered in the fight!
And yet once more our tongues can tell the triumph of the right;
And humbled is the haughty foe, who our destruction sought,
For God's right hand and holy arm have great deliverance wrought.
Oh, then, unto His holy name ring out the joyful song—
The race has not been to the swift, the battle to the strong.

On to Richmond.

After Southey's *"March to Moscow."*
By
John R. Thompson, of Virginia.

Major-General Scott
An order had got
    To push on the columns to Richmond;
For loudly went forth,
From all parts of the North,
The cry that an end of the war must be made
In time for the regular yearly Fall Trade:
Mr. Greeley spoke freely about the delay,
The Yankees "to hum" were all hot for the fray;
The chivalrous Grow
Declared they were slow,
And therefore the order
To march from the border
    And make an excursion to Richmond.
Major-General Scott
Most likely was not
Very loth to obey this instruction, I wot;
In his private opinion
The Ancient Dominion
Deserved to be pillaged, her sons to be shot,
    And the reason is easily noted;
Though this part of the earth
Had given him birth,
And medals and swords,
Inscribed with fine words,
    It never for Winfield had voted.
Besides, you must know that our First of Commanders
Had sworn, quite as hard as the Army in Flanders,
With his finest of armies and proudest of navies,

To wreak his old grudge against Jefferson Davis.
Then "forward the column," he said to McDowell;
 And the Zouaves, with a shout,
 Most fiercely cried out,
"To Richmond or h—ll" (I omit here the vowel),
And Winfield, he ordered his carriage and four,
A dashing turn-out, to be brought to the door,
 For a pleasant excursion to Richmond.
Major-General Scott
Had there on the spot
A splendid array
To plunder and slay;
In the camp he might boast
Such a numerous host,
As he never had yet
In the battle-field set;
Every class and condition of Northern society
Were in for the trip, a most varied variety:
In the camp he might hear every lingo in vogue,
"The sweet German accent, the rich Irish brogue."
The buthiful boy
 From the banks of the Shannon,
Was there to employ
His excellent cannon;
And besides the long files of dragoons and artillery.
 The Zouaves and Hussars,
 All the children of Mars,
 There were barbers and cooks
 And writers of books,—
The chef de cuisine with his French bills of fare,
And the artists to dress the young officers' hair.
And the scribblers all ready at once to prepare
 An eloquent story
 Of conquest and glory;
And servants with numberless baskets of Sillery,
Though Wilson, the Senator, followed the train,
At a distance quite safe, to "conduct the champagne:"
While the fields were so green and the sky was so blue,

There was certainly nothing more pleasant to do
  On this pleasant excursion to Richmond.
In Congress the talk, as I said, was of action,
To crush out instanter the traitorous faction.
In the press, and the mess,
They would hear nothing less
Than to make the advance, spite of rhyme or of reason,
And at once put an end to the insolent treason.
There was Greeley,
And Ely,
The bloodthirsty Grow,
And Hickman (the rowdy, not Hickman the beau),
And that terrible Baker
Who would seize on the South, every acre,
And Webb, who would drive us all into the Gulf, or
Some nameless locality smelling of sulphur;
And with all this bold crew
Nothing would do,
While the fields were so green and the sky was so blue,
  But to march on directly to Richmond.

Then the gallant McDowell
Drove madly the rowel
  Of spur that had never been "won" by him,
In the flank of his steed,
To accomplish a deed,
  Such as never before had been done by him;
And the battery called Sherman's
  Was wheeled into line,
While the beer-drinking Germans,
  From Neckar and Rhine,
With minie and yager,
Came on with a swagger,
Full of fury and lager,
  (The day and the pageant were equally fine.)
Oh! the fields were so green and the sky was so blue,
Indeed 'twas a spectacle pleasant to view,
  As the column pushed onward to Richmond.

Ere the march was begun,
In a spirit of fun,
General Scott in a speech
Said this army should teach
The Southrons the lesson the laws to obey,
And just before dusk of the third or fourth day,
  Should joyfully march into Richmond.

He spoke of their drill
And their courage and skill,
And declared that the ladies of Richmond would rave
O'er such matchless perfection, and gracefully wave
In rapture their delicate kerchiefs in air
At their morning parades on the Capitol Square.
But alack! and alas!
Mark what soon came to pass,
  When this army, in spite of his flatteries,
Amid war's loudest thunder
Must stupidly blunder
  Upon those accursed "masked batteries."
Then Beauregard came,
Like a tempest of flame,
To consume them in wrath
On their perilous path;
And Johnston bore down in a whirlwind to sweep
  Their ranks from the field
  Where their doom had been sealed,
As the storm rushes over the face of the deep;
While swift on the centre our President pressed.
  And the foe might descry
  In the glance of his eye
The light that once blazed upon Diomed's crest.
McDowell! McDowell! weep, weep for the day.
When the Southrons you meet in their battle array;
To your confident hosts with its bullets and steel
'Twas worse than Culloden to luckless Lochiel.
Oh! the generals were green and old Scott is now blue,
And a terrible business, McDowell, to you,
  Was that pleasant excursion to Richmond.

Rappahannock Army Song.
By
John C. M'Lemore.

The toil of the march is over—
  The pack will be borne no more—
For we've come for the help of Richmond,
  From the Rappahannock's shore.
The foe is closing round us—
  We can hear his ravening cry;
So, ho! for fair old Richmond!
  Like soldiers we'll do or die.

We have left the land that bore us,
  Full many a league away,
And our mothers and sisters miss us,
  As with tearful eyes they pray;
But this will repress their weeping,
  And still the rising sigh—
For all, for fair old Richmond,
  Have come to do or die.

We have come to join our brothers
  From the proud Dominion's vales,
And to meet the dark-cheeked soldier,
  Tanned by the Tropic gales;
To greet them all full gladly,
  With hand and beaming eye,
And to swear, for fair old Richmond,
  We all will do or die.

The fair Carolina sisters
  Stand ready, lance in hand,

To fight as they did in an older war,
  For the sake of their fatherland.
The glories of Sumter and Bethel
  Have raised their fame full high,
But they'll fade, if for fair old Richmond
  They swear not to do or die.

Zollicoffer looks down on his people,
  And trusts to their hearts and arms,
To avenge the blood he has shed,
  In the midst of the battle's alarms.
Alabamians, remember the past,
  Be the "South at Manassas," their cry;
As onward for fair old Richmond,
  They marched to do or die.

Brave Bartow, from home on high,
  Calls the Empire State to the front,
To bear once more as she has borne
  With glory the battle's brunt.
Mississippians who know no surrender,
  Bear the flag of the Chief on high;
For he, too, for fair old Richmond,
  Has sworn to do or die.

Fair land of my birth—sweet Florida—
  Your arm is weak, but your soul
Must tell of a purer, holier strength,
  When the drums for the battle roll.
Look within, for your hope in the combat,
  Nor think of your few with a sigh—
If you win not for fair old Richmond,
  At least you can bravely die.

Onward all! Oh! band of brothers!
  The beat of the long roll's heard!
And the hearts of the columns advancing,
  By the sound of its music is stirred.
Onward all! and never return,

Till our foes from the Borders fly—
To be crowned by the fair of old Richmond,
As those who could do or die.

Ashes of Glory.
by
A. J. Requier.

Fold up the gorgeous silken sun,
  By bleeding martyrs blest,
And heap the laurels it has won
  Above its place of rest.

No trumpet's note need harshly blare—
  No drum funereal roll—
Nor trailing sables drape the bier
  That frees a dauntless soul!

It lived with Lee, and decked his brow
  From Fate's empyreal Palm:
It sleeps the sleep of Jackson now—
  As spotless and as calm.

It was outnumbered—not outdone;
  And they shall shuddering tell,
Who struck the blow, its latest gun
  Flashed ruin as it fell.

Sleep, shrouded Ensign! not the breeze
  That smote the victor tar,
With death across the heaving seas
  Of fiery Trafalgar;

Not Arthur's knights, amid the gloom
  Their knightly deeds have starred;
Nor Gallic Henry's matchless plume,
  Nor peerless-born Bayard;

Not all that antique fables feign,
  And Orient dreams disgorge;
Nor yet, the Silver Cross of Spain,
  And Lion of St. George,

Can bid thee pale! Proud emblem, still
  Thy crimson glory shines
Beyond the lengthened shades that fill
  Their proudest kingly lines.

Sleep! in thine own historic night,—
  And be thy blazoned scroll,
A warrior's Banner takes its flight,
  To greet the warrior's soul!

Ask your bookseller for other Civil War related books from

BLUE MUSTANG

P R E S S

Several ongoing reprint series of historical texts will be available on an ongoing basis. Check your local or online bookseller or you can order direct from www.BlueMustangPress.com

www.ingramcontent.com/pod-product-compliance
Lightning Source LLC
Chambersburg PA
CBHW030110070426
42448CB00036B/611